Praise

for *Certain Women Called by Christ*

"God redeemed male and female on the cross of Calvary. God calls male and female servants into the ministry of God's church; and God has been using males and females in positions of sacred, servant, and spiritual leadership since God first spoke in the Book of Genesis. Human beings have come behind God and tried to make-over the subjects God created in His image into objects refashioned in the image of patriarchy and female inferiority.

Just as a grave could not hold Jesus in a borrowed tomb, the customs of male-dominated cultures have not been able to hold the truth that leaps off the pages of Luke's Gospel. Paige takes that truth and fashions a liberating work in this book that will bless those who recognize God's truth when they see it. Men and women will be freed from the prisons of cultural assumptions by the truth that Luke records and Dr. Chargois brings to readers' attention. This book is a must-read for all believers in Jesus Christ of Nazareth."

Rev. Dr. Jeremiah Wright
Senior Pastor, Trinity United Church of Christ, Chicago, Illinois

"A devout Christian, outstanding theolo~~~~ ~~~~~~~~~ ~~~~~~~~~
Dr. Chargois has studied the ~~~~~~~~ ~~~~~~~~~~
Here, she has written an outstar ~~~~~~~~~~~~~~~~
women in service to Christ, suj ~~~~~~~~~~~~~~~~~~
Bible."

Dr. Caroline L. Lattimore
15th Mid-Atlantic Regional Director & Centennial Membership Chairman, Alpha Kappa Alpha Sorority, Incorporated

"With great theological insight, Paige Chargois is able to bring these passages in Luke's Gospel to life with passion and sound biblical interpretation. Woven into these pages are some of the most insightful thoughts on the certain women surrounding Jesus."

Rev. Dr. Dwight C. Jones, Senior Pastor
First Baptist Church South Richmond

"The author gets to the heart of the matter to lift up that kernel of universal truth and substance that cuts through the noise and distraction of the world at large. Her book reassures us that all our lives have purpose, whether we showcase our talents in social, religious, educational, or political arenas."

Viola O. Baskerville, **Secretary of Administration**
Office of the Governor, Richmond, Virginia

"This wonderfully inspiring book is surely a must read—it nourishes your soul, inspires your heart, and feeds your spirit."

Carolyn C. W. Hines, Ed.D.
President, C. W. Hines and Associates, Inc.

"Paige Chargois's voice is vivid with lessons, thoroughly grounded in biblical verses, and powerful real-life experiences. This is engaging reading for the 21st century that engenders uniquely enriching spiritual exercises in the learning, unlearning, and re-learning of the Bible."

Dr. Tata Mbugua
Associate Professor, University of Scranton

"Dr. Chargois unearths the compelling stories of the women who responded to Jesus's call to accompany Him on His journey of ministry. Chargois is herself a *certain woman*, who long ago embarked on a similar spiritual journey, responding to God's call to be a risk taker and a world changer. She has found in these certain women the models of hospitality, service, courage, and creativity that will inspire both women and men to step out on the journey of faith in service to the Lord."

Rob and Susan Corcoran
Initiatives of Change/Hope In The Cities

"Passion and scholarship, challenge and sometimes controversy; Paige Chargois brings to her new book elements characteristic of her ministry."

Michael Henderson
Author, *All Her Paths Are Peace: Women Pioneers in Peacemaking*

"Chargois demonstrates that the early ministry of Jesus Christ involved *certain women*. More importantly, this book will propel modern day Christian women to answer the call and fully play their role in Christendom. This book will 'release' many, who had, hitherto, been held back due to inadequate interpretation of the role of women in ministry. A must read for Christian and non-Christian women alike; indeed for men also."

Dr. Judith Robo Orogun
Professor of Communication and English, Community College
Jamaica, West Indies

"Paige Chargois has demonstrated that she is a spiritual force with which to be reckoned. Because of her scholarship, love for Christ, and love for the church, this is worth your time to read it."

Dr. Carolyn Gordon
Professor, Fuller Theological Seminary

"Paige Chargois's fresh look at the role of women in Christ's ministry is through a sharp literary lens, informed not by modern mores but by biblical scholarship and analysis."

Louise Seals
Managing Editor, Retired, *Richmond Times Dispatch*

"What is it about the *certain women* who make the world a better place? Chargois suggests common qualities and leads readers to think about those who positively affect the lives of others. Who are the *certain women* in your life?"

E. Dianne N. Watkins
Founder, Chairman, and President, Bells for Peace, Inc.

"The Word of God is a two-edged sword with often the second edge left a bit rusty. In *Certain Women Called by Christ* author Paige Chargois polishes both edges. With her in-depth study, she helps readers see truths about God's call to women that we often ignore. She draws our attention to an edge worth polishing."

Martha Rollins
President/CEO, Boaz & Ruth

"Chargois has lifted the *truth* within the writing of Brother Luke and put it on the 'bottom shelf' so *everyone* can grab it! Thank you for empowering kingdom workers with a breath of fresh truth!"

Pastor Anthony and Lady Sandy Payton
Come As You Are Community Church, SBC, Fort Wayne, Indiana

Biblical Realities for Today

Certain
women
called by Christ

Paige Lanier Chargois

Believe it!
Love it!
Live it!

Chargois

Jan '08

NEW HOPE
PUBLISHERS
BIRMINGHAM, ALABAMA

New Hope® Publishers
P. O. Box 12065
Birmingham, AL 35202-2065
www.newhopepublishers.com

New Hope Publishers is a division of WMU®.

Library of Congress Cataloging-in-Publication Data
Chargois, Paige Lanier, 1944-
 Certain women called by Christ : biblical realities for today / Paige
Lanier Chargois.
    p. cm.
 ISBN 978-1-59669-200-8 (sc)
 1. Christian women—Religious life—Textbooks. 2. Bible. N.T. Luke
VIII, 1-3—Textbooks. 3. Women in the Bible—Textbooks. I. Title.
 BV4527.C473 2008
 270.082--dc22
                        2007045289

ISBN-10: 1-59669-200-6
ISBN-13: 978-1-59669-200-8

N084128 • 0208 • 6M1

To Deacon Earlie Hayes Lanier,
a loving father,
who, from my childhood,
has always valued and validated
the presence of
the living Christ in me,
and who honors
the call of God on my life.

And it came to pass afterward, that he went throughout every city and village, preaching and shewing the glad tidings of the kingdom of God: and the twelve were with him, and certain women, which had been healed of evil spirits and infirmities; Mary called Magdalene, out of whom went seven devils, and Joanna the wife of Chuza Herod's steward, and Susanna, and many others, which ministered unto him of their substance.

—LUKE 8:1–3 (KJV)

contents

foreword

YOU'VE HEARD THE OLD ADAGE, "IT TAKES ONE TO KNOW ONE!" WELL, many women of great faith, around the globe, could have written this book about Luke 8:1–3. Yet this is not simply a cultural essay about strong women. It took *this* one, a woman of *faith*, Paige Chargois, to know and to capture the essence of Luke's intent. He lifted up these *certain women*, not to be controversial in his time—or in ours—but to reflect accurately on Jesus's actual ministry.

Luke 8:1–3 is a minor text with a major message for today. *Certain Women Called by Christ* explains this text with depth and theological coherence and without any semblance of defensiveness for the cause of women. Luke's text is so clearly stated that any appearance of belligerence on the author's part is unnecessary. Paige Chargois simply sets forth biblical truth, as she also reminds us of biblical realities for today. Hers is a treatise celebrating Jesus's ministry, calling forth believers of both genders—equally—to hear, experience, and proclaim the good news of the gospel.

As these *certain women* moved from suffering to service and to celebration, so has this author. Her pen is filled with the ink of experience. She is intimately aware of the workings within the church and the work of the church, having come to Christ in her early childhood, and walking with Him in the present. Not only do the depth of her Christian spirit and the maturity of her faith merit your readership, but the breadth of this author's world travels and the scope of her academic training that combine to bring forth this fruitful work do also. She has become what she writes and speaks to proclaim.

This book will help the reader to gain a fresh view of the church and a renewed love for the work of the Master. We commend *Certain Women Called by Christ: Biblical Realities for Today* to all believers. Our hope is you will use this important book as an instrument through which even nonbelievers can experience the gentle touch of the Master's hand in their lives, just as He touched the lives of *certain women*.

Ella P. and Henry H. Mitchell

preface

CERTAIN WOMEN CALLED BY CHRIST EXPLORES AND EXPOUNDS ON three Bible verses that, too long overlooked by some and ignored by others, serve as a revelation into the life and ministry of Jesus then and now. The book challenges readers to see how Luke's Gospel affirms a truth that has often eluded many in the church: *certain women* were absolutely critical to the shaping of ministry in the newborn Christian community. The book goes on to reveal how today's *certain women* are critical to the shaping of ministry in and through Christ's body and to identify the biblical women's lifestyle characteristics to be modeled today.

Twelve descriptive realizations about these *certain women* leap—implicitly or explicitly—from the Luke 8:1–3 text and are the basis for the 12 individual chapters in this book. Each chapter provides illustrations of these realizations for application. In addition, reflective questions, for use in individual and group study, encourage women today to examine their lives at home, in the church, and in the world, to see how they are and can be *certain women.*

Appearing in the daily newspaper, the word *certain* would have little impact on us generally. However, as a pivotal word for Luke, *certain* resonates with meaning for us. Luke does not share loosely any word, phrase, or parable from or sequencing of Jesus Christ's ministry in his gospel presentation. From that perspective alone, Luke ratifies the importance of these *certain women.* A signature word for Luke, *certain* appears in Scripture (KJV) only 196 times, with 136 of those times in the New Testament, and 101 of those occasions emerging in Luke's writings alone. *Certain* is used 44 times in Luke's Gospel and 57 times in Acts. Most Bible commentators believe Luke penned Acts as well.

By contrast, the word occurs 10 times in Matthew and 11 times in Mark. John uses it only 5 times. This indicates Luke did not simply select the word from Matthew and Mark, though having used them as sources. *Certain* had greater significance for Luke than for the other Gospel writers. Luke identified a *certain* place where Jesus went to pray (11:1). *Certain women* meant at least two who could not be more closely defined; an indefinite quantity that is not without importance.

Each time used, the designation seems to have carried a sense of particularity: "a certain man" (8:27); "a certain centurion" (7:2); "a certain city" (5:12); "a certain lawyer" (10:25); "certain of the scribes" (20:39). Luke referred to *certain women* 5 times but only twice using his full phrase *certain women*: in 8:2 and at the Cross. The other occasions in which he used the term referenced individuals instead: "a certain woman named Martha" (10:38); "a certain woman" (11:27); "a certain poor widow" (21:2); "a certain maid" (22:56). Luke pointed to a plethora of other things or people. Well, you know a *certain* beggar (16:20) would have allowed most of Luke's readers to immediately envision a certain man at a certain spot in the marketplace, strategically standing to glean and garner the greatest number of coins tossed his way. A Pharisee; you know a *certain* Pharisee (11:37) would have stood out in people's minds among all of the Pharisees they may have known at the time, because that Pharisee would have distinguished himself in certain ways. Luke seemed confident his readers knew and comprehended his intent nestled within what is more of a general term to us.

How might this inform our thinking? These *certain women* were people that the community knew fairly well and no lengthy introduction was necessary. These were women who had already engaged Jesus in their needs. Jesus had healed, delivered, and cast out demons from their lives. So this moment was not the women's initial encounter with either most of the disciples or with Jesus Himself. Of all the people — or women — from whom Jesus had cast out demons, healed, or delivered, it was these *certain* ones whom He called forth to accompany Him and the Twelve on His journey of ministry! A word that at first may appear general to us should instead arouse interest; who were these *certain women* and how are they significant?

This book will help to raise awareness of these biblical women who were not left out on the fringe of the ministry. At the invitation of Jesus, these women became evidence of His tremendous power over death, hell, and the grave. They were critical, essential persons to be reckoned with as Jesus went from village to village sowing the seeds of the gospel to change the world!

These women were not on the fringe of spiritual fellowship nor excluded by Jesus from the ranks of religious leadership, as their individual biographies attest. Their inclusion becomes a vignette through which a stronger model of joint service, mutuality, and cooperation in the promulgation of the gospel can be enjoyed and competitive human behaviors in the church minimized today.

Few of these *certain women* have even been acknowledged fully throughout Christian church history. This book serves to identify them and glean the meaning their lives might have for ours. Despite anonymity, historically and today, *certain women* have been diligently pulling together community resources and pouring their own personal resources into various ministries. In these latter years, many *certain women* have grown their ministries from zilch to rare zeniths of accomplishments. They have not necessarily increased in personal wealth but, through sacrifice, have been tremendously blessed by God, who called and continues to call *certain women* into service.

acknowledgments

THE ABILITY TO SAY "THANKS" SEEMS TO BE STEADILY DIMINISHING IN these later generations, but it pleases me so to hear my 91-year-old father say, "Thank you" even for having passed him just a napkin across the table or having remembered for him where he left his watch the night before. He is the first one who taught me to say, "Thank you," and after 91 years, those words are still as fresh in his memory as the day when his mother (probably) taught him.

That sense of gratitude, spread over my lifetime, brings to mind a myriad of people I should thank, whose names, if listed individually, would probably fill another book of this size! Glancing back, God truly worked in mysterious ways! The true "Genesis point" is not *way back when* but in the more recent months when God basically said — through a series of events — that the time is *now*: From speaking at a conference in Virginia Beach, and having dinner with Woman's Missionary Union (WMU) consultant Debra Berry, I would be invited to a conference in Birmingham, which precipitated an invitation by WMU Executive Director Wanda Lee to address the WMU Convention in Greensboro, North Carolina, where New Hope's Publisher, Andrea Mullins, would simply pose the question to me, "When am I going to get your book?" Shocked out of my literary lethargy, I promised her the required proposal by my birthday, July 18. Without that affirming moment, this book would probably still be on my to-do list. I am deeply grateful to New Hope Publishers for its process and patience in bringing *Certain Women Called by Christ* to fruition.

Beyond the more obvious individuals on the pages of endorsements, others, who in particular and sometimes peculiar ways—their words, the timing of their questions, their encouragement, even just their wondering out loud to me about "a book"—have left indelible marks on my life. From Pastor Watson's, "When are you going to write your book?" to Sarah Smith's, "Paige, you ought to write a book on that!" to many others who have egged me on with their pronouncement, "Let me know when you write your book!"

Joyous gratitude is offered to each one who has endorsed the book. You have had a tremendous impact upon my life: academically, spiritually, socially, and professionally.

To those *certain women* whom I recognized as leaders in my early years and who influenced me not only to pledge the Alpha Kappa Alpha sorority in college but also to profoundly experience a quality of sisterhood, I say, "Thank you!"

In the throes of all that has occurred in my life, the world's greatest neighbor, Claudine Lee, has never let me forget that this book was something I had to do and would do in due time! Her words—and the cryptic/humorous way they were often said—that helped to keep me focused on God's future for me were, "It's gonna be aw'right!" And often laughter would follow the tears.

To the international Initiatives of Change/Hope in the Cities, I am deeply grateful for having served with you for nearly 20 years. There is a song I heard, *"The World Walked into My Heart."* Working with Hope in the Cities ushered in a greater quality of love for God's people all over the world and helped to hone my skills in making this world a better—more reconciled—place for us all! As we would often say, "What a journey!!!"

To Sister Beatrice Magette, I would like to say, "What tremendous honor you deserve. She has been to me a mother, a sister, a pastor, a friend, and a source of continual encouragement and Christian love. She herself is a *certain woman*—with a faith so alive and beautiful that she reflects every quality espoused in this book! Oh how we enjoy talking almost daily about our walk with the Lord. To you I say, "Thank you for being *on the journey!*

To Sister Ernestine Dawes and Dr. Samuel Roberts who offered their editing expertise and to the Drs. Henry and Ella Mitchell who—after "adopting" me as their own—simply kept me on their "short" prayer list, I say, "Thank you!"

Lastly, to the many unnamed people whose lives—and influence in my life—contributed so much to the vignettes I've shared in this book, "I offer my thanks to you for being who you were and are to me and for all that you helped me to become."

Paige Lanier Chargois

introduction

Having read through, over, and around Luke 8:1–3 in many years of biblical study, I eventually discovered this Word and wondered why I had never heard it referenced in any sermon I could recall. In its brevity, these verses not only identify a few specific, individual women, but connect with Jesus's ministry "many" other women who were part of His more than three-year blessed journey of service here on the earth!

Having been told numerous times that there were no women "in the Twelve," I have grieved that such a prominent text could be so lightly regarded and so profoundly disregarded. This text puts the whole human face on the ministry of Jesus: male and female; Jesus not only chose both to embody His ministry but needed both to carry out the tasks of spreading the gospel. God also inspired Mark to make note of the women (Mark 15:40–41*a*).

The Lord drew me to Luke 8:1–3 as I prepared to introduce Deacon Phyllis Taylor as a speaker at a church banquet. Thinking of her now refreshes the excitement engendered by Luke's text many years ago! This Scripture not only appropriately affirmed the influence of *certain women* in biblical times, but also, as I prepared to make observations about the speaker, I recognized the continuing reality of the influence of *certain women* today.

Deacon Taylor's service confirms her identity as a *certain woman* in the church today. Her presence is often felt far more than noticed. There is something quietly different about her, something deeply spiritual and serene. Nothing shakes her, even in the midst of tumultuous meetings. With each encounter, you are left with little doubt about her spiritual strength. She does not need to rule. She leads.

I had been given a brief biography about her, and I knew her personally. (We have a mutual love for the annual Christmas celebration. No corner of her house is unaffected by her decorative touch in celebrating the birth of our Lord. She is a collector of angels. I feel as though she makes them all bow and sing and flap their wings to give glory to the newborn King!) I knew I had to go "off the page" to declare what else needed to be said about Deacon Taylor: inspiring admiration and suffering jealousies of different intensities . . . never giving in to either, persevering in spite of and in the face of naysayers and human hindrances of all kind . . . a woman of means, married, and retired.

Like the *certain women* in Luke's text and Deacon Taylor, you and I have nothing to prove and everything to validate for ourselves. God's Word is God's Word. As believers, we cannot accept the parts we like and reject the parts we either don't like or find difficult to accept. Either God's Word has authority for us or does not have. Recognizing biblical realities that for too long have been "hidden" or ignored is one of the greatest cures to many inappropriate religious behaviors and attitudes today.

Certain Women Called by Christ is no feminist rewrite or retrograde theological musing. It's a fresh unearthing of a biblical text that has been buried under centuries of denial, disavowal, and disbelief—a celebration of the truth. It is no wonder this Scripture has been so easy to ignore. It's overshadowed by the anointing of Jesus at the end of Luke 7 and Jesus's presenting of Himself as the Sower of God's Word into human hearts that follows in Luke 8.

Yet Luke 8:1–3 is the text secure in giving to the church supporting biblical substance that women were part and parcel of the ministry of Jesus Christ. These *certain women* sought neither to diminish the ministries of the apostles nor usurp their apostolic status. Yet, early in Jesus's ministry, these women learned and were given the capacity to leave all and follow Him, changing the world then and now. The illumination of this Scripture serves to raise awareness in the study of the New Testament and deepen spiritual insight and assurance. Acceptance of the unambiguous declarations of this text serves to greatly reduce hostility between genders and generations and to reject the polarization of women in the church. That's worth celebrating!

My desire is not to provide theological arguments over this biblical text or around gender issues, or to shore up support for a feminist thesis by way of extrabiblical material. Rather, my desire is to connect believers with a text whose resonance—and, I believe, reason for existence—is to encourage spiritually, enable, and empower Christian believers for generations to come.

The rare and precious love for all of His disciples—to each who will hear—is the power of *Certain Women Called by Christ*.

Paige Lanier Chargois

certain women are not afraid to make history

How many times have we put on brakes at the brink of a major decision in our lives, utterly petrified of *falling into oblivion* or, more accurately, drowning in unknown or untested waters? How many times have we feared stepping onto unpaved paths we imagined no foot had trod? Equally afraid of setting a precedent, often we have allowed our questions about our abilities to die on the vine of latent inquiry as we shut down emotionally because of a negative chorus, such as, "We've never done that before!"

Women often have been pushed into patient "waiting 'till some other time" or shunted into silent graves of wishful thinking. Women have allowed fear to erode powerful capabilities to make history, falling into that role by default rather than with great intentionality. Rosa Parks comes to mind. Though that stance has begun to change significantly, there is still much distance to cover through courage and fortitude as women yet face the untried, untested, and yet-to-be-known futures that lie ahead of us all.

How often have we negated a great idea that bubbled up in our gray matter? How often have we thought, *Oh, they'll never let me do that!* Or worse yet, *If only* . . . . Each attitude is a graveyard for hopes and dreams that would otherwise birth different lives. At

> The Lord more than deserves our undivided attention, and we already have His!

times, bereft of that adventuresome spirit, women have watched as many brand-new possibilities for tomorrow slipped into the forgotten past of yesterday.

But *certain women* are not afraid to make history. *Certain women* are not incapable of gleaning necessary resources to make dreams come true. Mere wishful thinking is not nourishment for the souls of *certain women*. For them, stepping into the unknown enlarges their capacity to manage whatever might come their way. How? Through the faith and courage that *certain women* don't need to muster up. Rather, they possess this faith and courage out of due diligence: They have nurtured their faith in the quiet moments with the Master, and this faith in Him sustains them in the more difficult moments they eventually face. They insure their faith is nurtured in engagement of the living Lord *through prayer*, and they strengthen their faith in *diligent study* of and meditation on His Word.

Real prayer. This is not simply *thinking about* the Lord—for example, as one might do when driving along a highway. Nor is prayer talking *at* the Lord, never waiting for His response. Real prayer is *talking to the Lord* and *listening* attentively for what He says. The Lord more than deserves our undivided attention, and we already have His! Even on a human level, it's not easy to engage in a conversation with a person distracted by other issues. Folks who want appropriate responses to their words must be willing to fully focus on what they are asking, sharing, or declaring.

Jesus, the Twelve, and *certain women* were fully engaged as they walked down the paths, roads, and highways from the city of Jerusalem to the towns of Galilee. They journeyed into town after town together—listening to one another, planning together, and focusing on that which was critical to His mission. Although these *certain women* were not the first women Jesus had encountered, they were the first ones invited into the work of His ministry according to Holy Writ.

They, like their male counterparts, were leaving all to follow Jesus. In the company of well-selected males, *certain women* stepped into the unknown future of an expected Messiah. It was far more than doing a little volunteering for a while and giving some of their time to do good deeds in the community. As were the Twelve, these women were tapped to help transform their day, and the days to come, in the process of turning this world upside down—for good—and making history to the glory of God!

So many voices, historical and contemporary, would speak loudly and clearly for them to stay home instead of going into the highways and byways with Jesus. Their responsibilities would have been no less than ours and their cultural and traditional restraints would have been far greater and more intense. Yet they went. They were upstanding women in their respective communities or, at least, women of means. They struck out from home, family, friends, businesses, and more.

They made history. Jesus turned their lives into legacies and helped to create irreplaceable moments to transform history in ways no one could ever again deny. They walked with the Lord Jesus Christ toward an unknown destiny—with 12 men they probably did not or barely knew. These women stepped into the unknown, assured of a power with which they were already acquainted: Jesus's power had already healed, delivered, and saved them. He had cast out demons from them. They knew Him. This was enough to make them leave everything else to follow Him, even if on a temporary basis.

being women of worth

I searched a Web site that offers individuals its video production capabilities to preserve and document memories. Though the work of no theologian, biblical scholar, or anthropologist, Joe Terry's "*Making History*" site suggests we have special occasions videotaped to secure memories. He offers:

> *To preserve and document the memories of today for the benefit of tomorrow. Your life. Your business. Your legacy. Irreplaceable moments. Emotion and memory, transformed into a history only you can create, but that many will appreciate for a lifetime and beyond.*
>
> *We need to heal the wounds that we see and feel in society today. The wounds of a loss of shared history. We're moving so fast that we forget where we came from—the soul connections.*

The site includes this poignant quote attributed to Elias Lieberman: "Memories are all we really own."

Luke's *certain women* were not trying to make history or ingratiate themselves to their generation or generations to come. Their obedience involved moments of raw faith, powerfully conveying the simple truth of following Jesus: He is worth it—no matter the sacrifices, circumstances, or one's other hopes and dreams.

What God pours into our lives is of far greater value and consequence than present circumstances—divine value and consequence that not only shape and enlarge our very souls but also provide something substantive to bequeath to future generations and the whole world. When we walk and talk with Jesus, God enriches us personally as well as those we encounter.

Certain women, to connect with Jesus, responded to His invitation to journey with Him and the 12 disciples. Though secure and properly accommodated—if they had only Jesus, and if they had only a rock for a pillow—they risked their reputations and everything precious to themselves. There were, indeed, strong sociological boundaries between men and women. If they recognized Jesus as Messiah and not as only a prophet, they would also have realized that God was no longer speaking *through* human beings, but that—in the flesh—God was speaking *to* them!

Do you think they may have been afraid? Well, consider yourself in their circumstances. Jesus had begun to make Himself known. Yet many towns He entered had never heard His name. Many people opposed His ministry and some wanted to kill Him (Mark 14:1–2). Yet the women responded.

Making history doesn't come easily because so many things can make us miss the rare moments within which history is conceived. Those moments we later look back on and think, *If only I had ... thought differently ... reacted differently ... known better ... made a different choice*, and so on. We've all had them. However, such reflections should prepare us to become more sensitive and responsive to moments yet to come because history making is not over. Jesus still has the church in a life-changing, world-changing mode. Life lived through faith can offer exceptional opportunities.

From time to time, there are opportunities "to be the first" to go where none or few others have previously gone. Fearful thoughts may strike, but should not paralyze us and prevent our forward movement. Rather, we can remain on the alert for what a friend of mine calls "a God-sized assignment." Such is the life of those who are called to make history. Rather than a stagnating force, fear can be a catalyst we learn to use as a stimulus to accomplish great things in life!

The greatness of God always calls us to do that which we are unready or incapable of doing alone, because God has always anticipated and expected that we would not only need His help and power but also deeply desire it and learn how to tap into it to accomplish exceptional feats of which history books are written. No less is true for any believer. Especially, no less is true for *certain women* whose names are recorded in Holy Writ and subsequent annals of history.

We know we're about to make history, not because of the demands or impetus of ego, but when we find few if any models or capable mentors to help prepare us along the way. History is to be made through the God-sized assignments that He beckons us towards as part of the destiny for which He created us. Yet we can read history and learn what has already happened, deepen our faith, and ask Him to use us to make the history for which we were born—and born again—to accomplish! God has given us Luke's *certain women* to provide us with useful historical models. They certainly have been my mentors.

In my mind, two things can launch us into making history. The first is passion; the second is possibility. In life, we experience a passion for or against something. That passion prompts us to move in a direction with fiery determination. Yet others may not experience such passion; rather a possibility or happenstance might serendipitously open a door of opportunity that he or she must choose to walk through. Harriet Tubman had a passion for freedom—for herself and others—while Jackie Kennedy and Corretta Scott King encountered horrific happenstances in which they not only grieved for their slain husbands but became historic examples for the nation as they maintained discipline and dignity in extremely difficult circumstances. Life gave them possibilities. They gave to those possibilities a quality of human discipline and dignity that made history.

stepping out in faith

In 1999, I had the opportunity to journey to the Republic of Benin, West Africa. Initially, I felt no compulsion to attend the conference being offered by Benin's president, Mattieu Kerekou. All my life, academically and culturally, I had been told that no Africans sold other Africans into slavery; only Europeans "snatched" Africans from the shores of the motherland. If that were true, then President Kerekou's "apology" was suspect, to say the least. Additionally, West Africans had no written records during the era of slavery—only an oral tradition—so on what basis was his apology being given?

Little did I know then how complete were the Europeans' records. Where big money is being made, you had best believe there's a record somewhere! I convinced myself to go, finally deciding I did not want to miss that historic moment for Kerekou—whether true or not. The world was about to reach some level of certainty one way or another.

Benin's hospitality was grand and gracious. President Kerekou was ready not only to welcome the world to Benin but also to make an official apology to the world on behalf of any and all African nations that had participated in selling Africans to European traders. He had the evidence, from African tribal history to the written records of the Europeans. Historic revelation had ushered in world-class repentance.

Attending that conference was one of those moments I had almost let slip by in my life, not for what it offered me but for what it opened up to the world — much that, though hoped for, could not be seen at the time. It wasn't that the occasion didn't pique my interest or that visiting another part of the motherland wasn't sufficiently inviting. It simply wasn't a great priority in my life at that moment. In addition, it conflicted with what I had been assured of all my life. I went . . . and the rest is history.

That moment connected me with a special opportunity in Liverpool, England, and with a special sculptor with whom I would work along with others to "give birth" to something incredible for our world. We know of the horrific slave trade primarily between Liverpool, West African countries, and the Americas; a triangle of historic proportions. Such trade in priceless human lives is well documented. That was a "triangle" that separated and devastated humanity — sin that still taints our societies, sin that haunts and torments people of good conscience. However, many are yet to learn about the Triangle of Reconciliation that has sought to create an overlay of forgiveness upon the relational carnage of the past.

Benin began with a confession. Liverpool followed with declaration of its own participation. That precipitated an apology from Liverpool's 100 city councilors. Richmond, Virginia, under the tutelage of Hope in the Cities, had begun its Walk through History as a new way to acknowledge the historical hurts of others. Out of this flowed its Call to Community, through which a series of dialogues about race, reconciliation, and responsibility would be based. On staff with Hope in the Cities, I was already part of the work of racial reconciliation but had nearly missed my grand opportunity to help make history!

Standing in the sculpting studio of renowned British artist Stephen Broadbent, I heard the story about his fractured relationship with a dear personal friend. His pain would guide his artistic hands to sculpture an embrace that would subsequently be felt around the world! This sculpture would initially be placed in three British cities seeking to build new relationships with each other, healing some of England's own internal historic pain. Then it would move onto the world stage and be offered to the country of Benin in light of its apology to the world — a world filled with racial hatred and contempt that Liverpool (perhaps more than any other European city) had helped to create and from which the city had vastly profited.

In that moment, I did not perceive that I would help make history. It simply seemed to be the right thing to do . . . the normal next step. And I was quite surprised that no one else had thought of or contemplated how to make it happen. Something was "born" or "planted" within me in an embryonic moment from which the world would ultimately benefit. Internally, the light went on; externally, I declared these words: "Well, the trade and trafficking were not only between Africa and England; the Americas were quite involved as well [a fact we all knew but, before that moment, had not acknowledged]. Why not put a statue as well in the Americas?"

Broadbent welcomed the prospect, but we both knew some major hurdles lay before us to make it happen. Yet it did happen seven years later! In Richmond, Virginia, at Fifteenth and Franklin streets, a monument stands as a directional guide to a more glorious future of reconciliation for every person and group on whose lives hatred in any form has had a negative impact.

striding with God's truth

Carpe diem is the Latin term for "seize the day" or "grab the moment." The phrase awakens in us a greater preparedness to know which moments to seize. However, many missed cues occur when and if one is not walking the journey of faith with the Lord. *Carpe diem* might be wonderful for lighting on great opportunities, but the term has no power of its own to enable us to know what to do with the opportunities or enable us to persevere towards an appropriate culmination of the opportunity.

Journeying—fully engaged—with the Lord Jesus Christ *does* provide each of those priceless ingredients of His Spirit helping us to discern the moment, His strength carrying us until we eventually reach our goal, and His empowerment filling us with what it takes to bring opportunity to blessed culmination. In Him, fear is diminished and history is made. We cannot know our end from our beginning. Only as we walk with the God who declares, "I am the Alpha and the Omega, the Beginning and the End" (Revelation 21:6) can we launch fearlessly into the moments of our lives that will open doors to opportunities that create and sustain our personal legacies and bring historical realities that do ultimately bless our world.

Long before the Benin journey, God awakened something else in me that is part and parcel of *certain women* and their ability to make history. It is another journey that must take us all the way back to the Garden of Eden. We cannot get our future straight if we don't rightfully reckon with our past. For me, this was my "journey from the beginning," because I felt compelled to understand anew what God intended for me.

It was fall 1979 when I was in Louisville, Kentucky. I had begun my second semester in seminary. A particular pastor invited me to join with his church and to help him do several specific tasks. Beyond what he asked of me as a regular member, I joined the choir and a choir committee preparing for the upcoming Women's Day celebration. Eventually, the choir members wanted me to participate in the program by also saying a few words about the songs in our miniconcert. I agreed and began learning the songs along with the other choir members, meditating on the lyrics, and also writing a three-minute commentary for the worship portion of the celebration service.

On Women's Day, immediately following my commentary, the people in the congregation arose to their feet in joyous confirmation and agreement. Yet evidently, this response was in direct opposition to what the pastor felt and believed! My final words had merely been these:

> *Although God made woman second in time, that was never to mean that God made woman second best.*

The pastor, though withholding comment then, disagreed with my statement (though I still believe the Bible solidly reflects what I said).

I later learned that he saw my statement as vaunting woman's position *above* man's. I thought it clear the content and intent of my brief message were this: What God made and called woman was never intended by God to be made into a second-class citizen within His great creation. Being reminded that Scripture is clear—God made nothing else after He made woman—suggests creation was complete. Nothing else was needed except the obedience of those whom God had created. Man was the bedrock of God's creation, but woman was definitively the crowning touch of that same creation (Genesis 2:18, 22).

Long after the fall of man and woman (Adam and Eve), Jesus finally reunited the two in God-ordained ministry on His journey to bring salvation, healing, and deliverance in ways that would glorify God as Creator and Sustainer of our world. Our God was not quite finished making history with, through, or for His creation. Is this not the same God who is yet working through men and women today? God compels us to understand our past so we can understand our future. He has specific intentions for our lives; He is equally concerned with the life of *every* human He creates—man and woman alike.

Who the
certain women
disciples
were, we can
become.

Who the *certain women* disciples were, we can become. What they accomplished, we can replicate. They bore within their bodies the power of His might and within their lives so great a testimony to the realness of the Christ! They were "something else" before He took them on His journey, and on the journey, they became something special to Him, to His ministry, to one another, to themselves, and now to us.

Leaving everything—no matter how temporarily—to serve His cause, they made history! When He "released" them to return to their homes and families, they were normal. Yet *normal* had new meaning, substance, and a transformative power that made their world new again. While the ordinariness of their lives continued after He departed, the extraordinariness of their witness became paramount: They had walked with the Lord as no other women had done and as few men had had the honor and privilege to do. We can walk with Him in this way, spiritually strong because of our relationship with Him.

eflections

Longfellow poetically described those who leave "footprints on the sands of time. . . ." Where have you chosen to leave your footprints for the glory of God and the blessing of God's people?

Where and when have you been given the opportunity to be "the first"?

What did you do with the opportunity?

What else could you do with the opportunity in order to build up others and to glorify God?

*P*rayer

certain women
pave the way

WE BREEZE ALONG ON BEAUTIFULLY CONSTRUCTED ROADS TO MYRIAD destinations, often oblivious to the tedious work others rendered in order to create these pathways for us. Others have successfully cut and shaped paths, layered the grit and gravel, steamrolled the tar, and then painted the yellow and white safety lines just so. Others' preparations guide our progress on the roads we travel.

Similarly, contemporary women may be nearly as oblivious to the other women who have paved the way for them in the church and ministry of our Lord! Others had the more tedious tasks of cutting the paths through the grit and gravel of negative attitudes about women in the church. Others attempted to smooth the way for greater female leadership and sharing of gifts and abilities. These others are often not recognized or affirmed, but overlooked if not discounted for their contributions to paving the way for contemporary women to do greater ministry.

Women in most professional fields—but more importantly women within the Christian faith—have had to endure the stresses of paving the way through a forest of religious ideas, as well as the peaks and valleys of theological insights and biblical pronouncements that negate them. We find such women in the eighth chapter of Luke; a couple of them the other Gospels never even mention. Yet Jesus values women; we are a special part of God's plan to open a highway for Him into the hearts of others. In a *Journal of Theology* article, "Why God Became Man: A Gender-Inclusive Christological Perspective," Wendy J. Deichmann Edwards uncovers the value of the *certain women* among Jesus's disciples by noting the practical and theological reasons for Jesus's gender. She concludes the following;

> *This [was] the most gender-inclusive incarnational arrangement possible and most fitting for a God who is neither male nor female. . . . If God had become enfleshed and revealed as a woman in first-century Palestine, there would have been severe practical problems with this arrangement. Primary ones are that almost no one would have noticed her and only other women would have listened to her. With no biological offspring, she would have had no children of her own to teach, let alone the religious crowd or the public.*

There would have been not only sociological stumbling blocks but also religious realities that would have been nearly impossible to change within three and a half years. That was the extent of Jesus's ministry. Surely, coming as female incarnate instead of male, Jesus "would not have been allowed to sit among the priests and elders to study the Law and the Prophets or to speak with or teach men," Deichmann Edwards concludes.

Almost no one would have noticed her.

Beyond those considerations would have been the sociological boundaries between men and women and the limitations women had established within their own relationships.

Deichmann Edwards continues,

> *If God had become enfleshed as a woman, what kind of impact would it have made upon men that she was uncompromisingly loving, respectful and forgiving, even to 'the least of these,' even unto death? Women were generally expected to act in these ways. So if Jesus had been a woman, would anyone, male or female, have detected an unusual sacrifice or example of relevance for men in her? If Jesus had been a woman, she would only have been allowed to approach and teach other women. God became man to reach both men **and** women. (emphasis added)*

Who were these women to us? Qualifying his *certain women* category, Luke names three women, and then casts a broad linguistic net as he refers to "many others," indicating at least more than two others—even a seemingly larger, innumerable group of women in addition to these he had placed on his biblical role of disciples in Jesus's entourage—although with a limiting sentiment suggested and nuanced by the word *certain*. They were of a *certain* quality or of a *certain* standing within the community or perhaps of a *certain* commitment that Jesus had ignited within them. They surely were of a *certain* quantity because so few were specifically named. Yet Luke knew there were more.

He seems to be simultaneously admitting his lack of knowledge of the extent of their existence while also declaring his assurance that they did, in fact, exist. They were not merely casual *followers*. They were a dedicated cadre who had been touched by Jesus's power.

His power had healed, delivered, and even cast out the demonic from their lives. Jesus had brought order out of chaos and refused to allow the waters of life to overwhelm the shores of their very souls. He had now invited them on the journey with Him and the Twelve to the many towns and villages in the region of Galilee! Instead of apparently reveling in any sense of being special, they simply prepared themselves for the departure—perhaps more cognizant of what they were *departing for* than what they were *departing from;* they had the very evidence of who He was within the healing He had wrought in their bodies and the deliverance He had brought to their lives!

They did not know the ramifications attached to what and whom they were leaving, but they must have had a great assurance that they had to help the world know of this One who had so profoundly changed who they were and even how they perceived themselves. On the way, they were probably quite naïve to the fact they were paving the way to new realities in the lives of men and for the lives of women. These *certain women* were truly paving the way, yet most likely had no clue of that peculiar task and destination. That was not part and parcel of their comprehensive image of themselves.

All they knew about themselves in the moment was that they had heard the voice of the Lord and were on the way to the cities and towns of Galilee with Him. Gladly, they would tell what He had done for them. They were on the journey to help spread the good news about who this Jesus is and could be in the lives of many folk they were sure to encounter. Seeking to serve Him as He forged ahead to build God's kingdom, they were simply being obedient to the very call of Christ.

Most often, *certain women* today do not intuit themselves as paving the way because they imagine other women have somehow already done this and that those women are farther down the road, perhaps out of sight around the bend of knowledge . . . way ahead experientially, while they themselves are almost bringing up the rear. Indeed, often women have labored and languished over—even waited until later in life to heed—the call to journey with the Master.

they were free, indeed

In *The Women Around Jesus*, author Elisabeth Moltmann-Wendel declares, "The coming of Jesus released new values . . . freed from old standards; new patterns of behavior . . . opened up to us." That Jesus had a unique relationship with women is nothing new. What is becoming newer all the time within successive generations is women's understanding of that new and unique relationship with the Son of God who became Savior of the world and their Risen Lord. This uniqueness is seen especially in Luke's Gospel; women are not just part of the crowd or simply among the general followers or believers. They are recorded as *certain women* who also are on a segment of the journey with Him to change the world!

For anyone, male or female, to have been enlisted into the service of the Savior was far more amazing as we glance back through historical, theological, and biblical telescopes. However, we celebrate the reality that is present in Luke's text that clearly and irrefutably sets forth the human underpinnings of Jesus's earthly ministry in the lives of both male apostles and *certain women* of His day—*both* carefully selected and both uniquely called.

Women have transitioned socially and politically over the past century. On parallel tracks, their understanding of themselves biblically and their fuller roles in God's kingdom have grown. The former, *some women* have passionately pursued. The latter *most women* of faith have often passively accepted.

However, though women have, to some degree, experienced new levels of responsibility, service, and leadership roles in the church, their biblical and spiritual self-knowledge has not often kept pace. Most women of faith have been more passive and patient in acknowledging the spiritual underpinnings of their newfound status in the church over the past 30 years.

At one point in my life, nearly 20 years ago, I was preparing to change denominations, bored to tears with irrational reasons for allowing my God-given gifts to go unused and sick nearly unto death (metaphorically speaking), over the harshness in the church I had experienced, with fewer men than women being the source. After much pain and prayer, having been accepted into a denominationally different seminary, in no uncertain terms, God prevented me from leaving Richmond to walk into my newly chosen denomination. Distraught and deeply disappointed, I soon saw the Comforter gently usher in God's revealed will for my life: remain Baptist.

And He did so with words spoken into my spirit: *I have given you life in a Baptist family. . . . I have given you salvation through a Baptist church. . . . I have trained you and honed your gifts under Baptist leaders. . . . I have called you into the service of the gospel through a Baptist pastor. . . . I have educated you in a Baptist seminary and called you into ministry.*

All I could do was bow and say, "Thank You, Lord!" But when I got up from my knees, I was spiritually compelled to connect who I was as a Baptist-believing female leader with a greater Christ-centered, biblical identity. I knew there were so few of us but had not comprehended the degree to which I had been chosen to pave the way. The joy of having been selected by the Lord was somewhat diminished by the pain encountered in just trying to utilize the gifts, training, and abilities He had given me. The strength of daily recommitments to the task of following the Master ameliorated that pain. This was in no way a rejection of other denominations who more readily welcomed females into ministry; it was an aspect of remaining faithful where God wanted me to serve regardless of the difficulties.

I hoped for him he could eventually place the emphasis where it really belonged: on the bread and wine.

To make this point more poignantly, around that time, I heard a pastor declare that communion might not be communion if it were given to him from the hands of a woman. Though I understood the painful spiritual struggle he was so publicly sharing, as a woman intensely listening to his verbally etched dilemma, I hoped for him that he could eventually place the emphasis where it really belonged: on the bread and wine itself. If the words of Jesus are definitive, He simply declared:

> *"Take and eat; this is my body." Then he took the cup, gave thanks and offered it to them, saying, "Drink from it, all of you. This is my blood of the covenant, which is poured out for many for the forgiveness of sins."*
> —MATTHEW 26:26–28

Biblically it mattered not about whose hands served communion: disciples and believers received it from one another as it was passed around the table. What mattered to Jesus was that those who did believe remember Him in this way, using what He used—bread and wine—to honor His body and the New Covenant that brought believers together with God through His sacrifice on the Cross.

Paving the way has not been easy. Through the years, everything about women in the church has been questioned, second-guessed, rejected, and outright denied! And yet, the road is much smoother now for believers, in general, and for those on the receiving end of great quality of ministry that women offer across this land and around the world. In paving the way, they have done no less than John the Baptist at the beginning of the ministry of Jesus: made straight the path for the Christ to enter the lives and souls of men and women all over the world.

But now women are beginning to see how they share in the incredible kingdom task of paving the way for souls to even hear the gospel and experience the same, powerful, soul-saving liberation that belonged to Mary, Joanna, Susanna, and *certain women,* such as Salome and many others. Women today are reconnecting with biblical female ancestors who paved the way spiritually, practically, and relationally. Though there has been disconnectedness assuredly.

Wrongly isolating Mary Magdalene as a prostitute over the centuries virtually eliminated her from our spiritual line of ancestors for so many years. The slur against her character, superimposed over her strong biblical image, defaced the reality of her profound deliverance. It minimized the scope of her service and leadership once the Master had "shut down" the demons that had harassed her. Likewise, we have been told and taught that biblical women had no resources of their own; we were misled with the thoughts of a near-total male financial domain. There is no doubt that some of these *certain women* were women from wealthy households. All of the women were devoted to the Lord, not their means.

they would follow Jesus anywhere

Mary Magdalene is acknowledged multiple times in the life and ministry of Jesus, beginning with the seven demons being cast out of her (Mark 16:9; Luke 8:2). She was present during Jesus's trials and sufferings (Matthew 27:45–56) and was quite near to Him at His death (John 19:25). She was the first to behold Jesus after His resurrection (John 20:15–16). The prominence of this *certain woman* in Jesus's life and ministry is indisputable and is to be appreciated and celebrated as Jesus severed her past and ushered her into a far more glorious future.

"The devotion of Mary Magdalene to her Lord is evident through her unending service to Him," according to the *Encyclopedia of Bible Characters*. Jesus appeared to Mary, who was moved to tears at His tomb and in great despair, having perceived that she had lost her Lord. It was only as Jesus spoke her name that she recognized Him (John 20:16). She knew Jesus well enough to not be fooled by any other voice. She then returned to the disciples, who were no strangers to her, exclaiming, "I have seen the Lord!" (John 20:18). Mary Magdalene was an extraordinary woman, lovingly devoted to her Lord in His life, death, and resurrection!

The *Encyclopedia of Bible Characters* also identifies Joanna as not only the wife of the man who managed Herod's household but also, as Luke reports, another woman healed by Jesus. She was the second one named who accompanied Jesus from Jerusalem to Galilee near the end of His earthly ministry. The Gospels declare that she was also one of the women present when Jesus was laid in the tomb (Luke 23:55–56) and one of those Jesus commanded to "go tell" after His resurrection (John 20:17). Though Joanna and the other women were not titled among the Twelve, they played significant roles. Significant and unique qualities reside within *certain women* who serve the cause of Christ, often without need or enjoyment of titles.

Don't get me wrong, titles are important and denote significant accomplishments and levels of both capability and commitment. However, as we focus on titled persons, we often forget or push to the background some great laborers in the kingdom who are without title. As an African American, I have helped to fight the battle for appropriate honor and respect for those who have titles—from just the basic social titles of respect (Miss, Mrs., and Mr.) to titles denoting academic accomplishment. As a woman, I have helped to fight the battle for women to have equal access to titles—and therefore opportunities. Yet I observe that, once titled, you realize the title doesn't make you who you are; you, as a *certain woman,* qualify and validate the title—whatever it may be.

There seemingly was no struggle for "entitlement" of any kind among these women who were invited on the journey with Jesus. In role clarification—if it came up—I imagine Jesus would have declared to these *certain women* some of what He had declared to Peter about John when Peter's sense of place, entitlement, or competitiveness with John got in the way of doing the work of the Master. Jesus responded, "If I want him to remain alive until I return, what is that to you?" (John 21:22).

In paving the way, these *certain women* were not free of troubles, heartaches, and pain. But they followed. Often because of their loyalty to Jesus Christ, such trouble, heartache, and pain compounded. However, how they seemingly handled these challenges distinguished these women—and continues to distinguish *certain women* today—from many other women. How God allows us to experience a depth of pain is often more than amazing.

More amazing is the reality that we continue to exist *beyond* the pain we've experienced. But we are not called just to *journey with* the Master but are called *unto* the Master who says, "Come unto me, all ye that labour and are heavy laden, and I will give you rest" (Matthew 11:28 KJV). His words continually cause us to reevaluate what and why we're doing what we're doing: "Take my yoke upon you and learn from me, for I am gentle and humble in heart, and you will find rest for your souls. For my yoke is easy and my burden is light" (Matthew 11:29–30).

These Scriptures belong to every believer. However, it seems that *certain women* tend to apply such Scriptures readily as they live with an awesome sense of immediacy in the Word of the Lord and with the Lord's Spirit; an immediacy that often leads to pain in our human relationships. Tapped as a public reader of Scripture in worship—someone who could readily pronounce even the difficult Old Testament names with ease due to having studied eight languages—I once asked the pastor if with careful discernment I could substitute the name *God* for the pronoun *He* when reading his selected texts in worship.

His immediate response was, "What's wrong, Paige? You don't like men or something?"

My immediate response was, "No, Pastor. It's because I love God and the listening believer!" I added that English overuses pronouns. In long translated sentences, often who the pronoun *He* refers to can get lost in the minds of listeners. The text becomes much more powerful if names are used somewhat more frequently rather than following the general English rule of just once in a sentence and then pronouns.

He consented, but also left me in pain that my love for God had to be immediately intuited as contempt for men. There was no confusion in me about my gender and no diminishing love and respect for men. Rather the source of my request had been a passionate desire to better communicate the Word of God so that, in the ear and mind of the hearer, there would be no confusion.

But God helps us to neither deny such pain that might be part of our past nor to denounce its power to continually afflict our present and affect a more glorious future to which He is calling us. Rather, God enables us to acknowledge such pain, embrace it, and know it is part of having "paved the way" for His gospel and His glory. The only way to sustain such focus is through an intimate, deeply devotional relationship with Jesus Christ. That provides to *certain women* what I call "close-up power"; power from the Lord to prevent any pain of the past from becoming an incessant, destructive tendency that robs hope, trust, and love. It requires a faith that is mature yet submissive to the Lord of life, in order to carry out His ministry on the earth.

they served Jesus through other trials

Women of means, these *certain women* were not just offering hospitality and refreshment on the road trips Jesus took with

His disciples. The *certain women* provided not only financial contributions, food, and sustenance but also a spiritual cocoon within which Jesus felt comfortable to be renewed for the next leg of the journey in the gospel. In his book, *Jesus of Nazareth*, Gunther Bornkamm puts it in perspective for us:

> *The people to whom he talks and with whom he deals are also there undisguised and real. They all contribute something towards the encounter with him. The righteous contribute their righteousness, the scribes the weight of their doctrine and arguments, the tax collectors and sinners their guilt, the needy their sickness, the demoniacs the fetters of their obsession and the poor the burden of their poverty. This encounter compels everyone to step out of his (or her) customary background. This bringing to light of men as they really are takes place in all stories about Jesus. It happens each time, however, simply and as a matter of course, without in any way being forced, without that awkward compulsion towards self-disclosure . . .*

You may wonder why it is that *certain women* pave the way? Every born-again believer experiences some difficulty as he or she becomes a new witness for the Lord. However, *certain women* experience additional difficulties outside the usual challenges, especially balancing home life with church life and, more critically, even learning to integrate, not just balance, the two. Why is it that *certain women* pave the way? It's because of the grit and gravel they experience while attempting only to be faithful to God's call upon their lives; it's because of the trials.

I recall the Sunday I was welcomed back home from seminary graduation by my pastor. A woman made her way to me immediately after worship and declared—with a bit of an attitude—"Now you're going to be up there with all the men." Naïve, I did not grasp what she meant and later simply realized that was some of the grit and gravel being thrown on the road for which God was using me to pave the way. In paving the way, we realize that God will use us to change people's minds about themselves, others, and even God! None of which should be deemed as easy. Sometimes it seems that, as *certain women,* we're even steamrolled. But be of great cheer! God is just paving new roads with our lives.

Reflections

Often we are willing to sacrifice for our own advancement but less so for the advancement of others. Which roads in life are you willing to clear with self-sacrifice in order to make it a little easier for others to live out a greater salvation and faith experience?

Which would be the most difficult for you to risk for the cause of Christ: your reputation, your life, your friends, or your family, and why?

Prayer

certain women
commit out of their own means

It is worth repeating. There is no doubt that these *CERTAIN women* were women of means, including women from wealthy households and women who had chosen to respond in great ways financially to Jesus Christ and His ministry. Luke is very clear that they gave "out of their own means." This suggests that they needed not to ask anyone for permission to support the ministry of the One who had healed and delivered them.

This would have been an awesome revelation to many believers of that day and is a revelation for us today: a brand-new sense of these *certain women* being valued by Jesus Himself. We have scant to no records of the contributions that came from these women of independent means. We see clearly that the Lord, having saved them and involved them in His ministry, not only changed their living, but profoundly changed their giving. How significant a reality that is within the ministry that gave birth to the Christian church!

This text would suggest that—giving behaviors in our churches today bear out this truth—our giving is more greatly in response to our *experiencing* the power and presence of the Christ than in only *believing* in Him. Although the practice of tithing can easily be taught by the church and supported by tenacious Bible study, the will to give is shaped more profoundly by one's experience of the Christ. This experience controls the degree to which new testimonies are shaped.

One *certain woman* in particular—Mary Magdalene—was a woman wrongly characterized as a prostitute. (Modern biblical scholars refute the characterization, though she *was* a person out of whom Jesus had cast seven demons [who knows what type].) Whatever her reputation, she still contributed to the ministry of Jesus, and her contributions were accepted. Evidently it was her chief desire to lavish the Christ and His ministry with her giving. It seems from Jesus's perspective that when deliverance occurred in her life, not only was she delivered of seven demons but demons—or the taint of sin—were ousted from her possessions as well.

they were radically changed to live afresh

The dramatic changes in Mary Magdalene's life radicalized all she possessed! She was brand-new, filled with new life, cleansed from old ways, behaviors, and sins, and enjoyed a quality of life that can only be described as born again! What she had left over from a life afflicted with the demonic became a life delivered.

Her ways of thinking were brand-new! Her ways of relating to others were brand-new! Her household and everything she possessed had the aura of being brand-new! Out of an old purse but a new heart, she gave to the work of the Son of God. Some of the other women or some of the Twelve may have silently questioned her contribution. Jesus didn't. He knew that she gave out of the treasure of her heart and not the coffers of her past. In Him, the past was gone. In Him, the present and future were what mattered. In Him this *certain woman* was, again, free indeed!

Joanna's means would have been unquestioned coming from a highly respected family as the wife of the king's treasurer. Her giving was unparalleled amongst the other women or even among the Twelve. But how many might have silently wondered about her motives? It seems evident, however, that Joanna did not need to depend upon her husband's income or on Herod's treasury from which she could draw out contributions to the Lord who had healed and delivered her. Luke declares she—as did the others—gave out of her own resources.

Jesus loosed their lives to be lived in fullest expression, to experience its deepest depths and its sublime accomplishments.

That she had monies over which she had authority was, again, instructive in biblical times and also for our contemporary times. The church historically had taught that women had little to any financial resources and, even if they did, women certainly were given no authority over such funds. There were so few exceptions to this scenario with only a couple of "women of means" or businesswomen identified in Scripture.

We have here two women at opposite ends of the social spectrum of life: one who had means but from whom seven demons had been cast out whereas the other was abounding in high society with a great reputation to match. Joanna thrived in a household provided by a man who loved her. There's no mention of Mary Magdalene's relationship with any man.

But they each could love Jesus the same, in response to His healing touch. Their lives were loosed and set free to be poured into

Jesus's life and ministry. These women's giving was a full surrender of all that they had in support to all that Jesus was to them.

Jesus loosed their lives to be lived in fullest expression, to experience life's deepest depths and its sublime accomplishments. Jesus also released their finances from every hindrance that would hold them back from contributing as He needed and as they, therefore, desired. Money was not to be stored and kept for times and needs afar off. Though obviously disciplined in the accumulation of some personal wealth, the *certain women* rose to a new quality of living and giving because of the power Jesus demonstrated in them personally. The *certain women* could have used their finances for a myriad of other things. But when they met Jesus, *things* no longer mattered! Their priorities changed. Their values changed.

they experienced a sweet surrender

Oh, that He could stir our hearts to such levels of giving to His life, ministry, and bride, the church. Rather than giving today in response to what the deacons, preachers, or missionaries ask for, our giving could be already on the level of surrendering our total selves and assets to the Christ, in order to be shared proportionately with how greatly He has blessed us. Our treasure—great or small—can help to resource the ministry of Jesus, who does not discount what we bring to Him.

Our priorities can change. Our values can change. Where we shop can change. What we shop for can change. No longer the cravings for designer names. *The Designer of the universe* through Jesus Christ wants us to "wear" His design in our hearts—the garments of deliverance, the design of a new person—and, as the seal covering our very souls, an everlasting assurance of His gift of salvation.

These *certain women* gave out of their own resources, as can we. The building of the kingdom takes precedence over both the past and the present so that everyone's future can be better. Depending upon our social and economic stations in life, we may not have equal deposits on hand, but what God values is giving out of the "deposits" He has placed in our hearts; not simply taking dollars from one account or another.

How many times have some of us perhaps had nothing but the "widow's mite" to put into the offering plate, whereas, at other times, we've had a greater amount to offer the Lord? In 1 Chronicles 29, David not only declared, "All things come of thee and of thine own have we given thee" (v. 14 KJV), but also that "both riches and honour come of thee " (v. 12 KJV). However, the most potent declaration of David's prayer is in verse 17 (KJV) where he captures the essence of our relationship with God—"I have willingly offered all these things: and now have I seen with joy thy people to offer willingly to thee."

Amazingly, our giving flows out of the depth of our experience with Christ but it also "seasons" and shapes our relationships with others. We are as close to God as we are to people! Here is a biblical text that seems to put that in perspective: the degree of willingness with which we offer ourselves and make our offerings to God shapes our ability to see God's people through the lens of joy instead of fear and trepidation, hostility or jealousy, contempt or hatred.

Our giving not only reflects that He has changed our hearts, but also reveals that our perspectives on others—in and out of the kingdom—are healthier. People, rather than becoming pawns in our hands to manipulate for our own benefit, pleasure, and vainglory, for example, are connected to us in unity. People cease to be competitors with whom we might compare our giving and service to the kingdom. Instead, we give out of our own resources and the resources of our heart so that other hearts can be changed radically. Like David, *certain women* can now see God's people "with joy"—not with envy, malice, a sense of competitiveness, or the arrogance of a one-upmanship spirit.

When Christ comes into our lives, not only does He change our hearts, but also He becomes for us the ultimate Source from whom all of our resources are drawn. He changes how we see our resources. Our resources become "bottomless" as we never run out of what we need and what sustains life and contributes beauty to our lives. Our bottom line is no longer an accounting sheet to show our net profit (within our new spiritual sensibilities), because all that we have is profit from God's hand.

His Word assures us of His capacity not only to supply our every need (Philippians 4:19) but also to even give us the desires of our hearts (Psalm 37:4). Yes, the present, pervasive power of the Lord—demonstrated by His deliverance—leaves no dimension of our lives untouched by His power nor untapped for His service! We are transformed not just in *what* we give but also in *why* we give, that is, out of which perspective we bring our resources to bear upon the work of His kingdom.

These *certain women* not only walked with him from Jerusalem to Galilee—going with Him into every city and village—but they also poured their finances into His ministry so that others could enter God's kingdom as well. Now it becomes laughable to ask, "Do I tithe on my gross or net?" It is a moot point. Why divide nickels and dimes when our focus should be on the richness and vastness of our salvation experience? It's not just that "everything belongs to God" already but that His giving to us in such an unrestrained way eliminates the harnesses on our giving to His kingdom and cause.

What Luke puts together is far more profound than "seed-giving" that's such a pervasive theme to many today. In that paradigm, we give to get! In Luke's paradigm, these *certain women* gave in response to the wealth they had already received from Jesus: healing, deliverance, and salvation.

What will change or condition our ways and sums of giving to the Lord? In the mind of this faith traveler, only a radical experience of the power of the risen Christ in our lives will change us individually from doling out a dollar or two at offering times to more properly gaining better stewardship over all of our resources so that we may give to the Lord all He requires and more! As in any relationship, our giving reflects our love. Part of the anger experienced in the church today, I believe, emanates from a conflict in our relationship with the Lord between the "quality" of our worship and the "quantity" of the offerings that we bring. We cannot be full of praise, sincerely, while remaining "empty" of our tithes and offerings. The decibels of our praise cannot camouflage the "tinkling cymbal" of our offerings.

Too often, our giving hardly reflects the level of blessings Christ has poured into our lives, even within the past week! It would seem to me that for Luke to mention that these *certain women* contributed out of their own means is significant for two reasons beyond their being women of independent means: He knew what the law required, and he had never commented on any offering brought by the Twelve. The women's giving, therefore, must have been significant relative to the giving of others within the "in crowd" on the journey of ministry.

It is easy to hide our giving. Today offerings are "hidden" because we just drop them in the basket or plate, putting our envelopes in blank side up. And church financial records are often relatively private.

The question is not about whether we hide our actual offerings but at what level of spiritual maturity will we choose to live? We cannot live on one spiritual level through our faith and feelings and on an entirely different level when it comes to our finances. Many Christians are in significant spiritual conflict (inner turmoil) today because of this inequity: we find it easy to declare that we love the Lord but quite difficult to just contribute to His kingdom even ten cents on a dollar for starters. That's the beauty of Luke's accounting declaration that "they supported him out of their own means." The level of support, I would believe, was proportionate to the blessings they enjoyed and not simply their financial well-being. Their giving was out of gratitude for lives changed, lives empowered, lives healed, indeed, lives delivered and made whole.

As long as you know and God knows what you are actually giving, that is all that matters, because what flows from obedience is joy and what flows out of disobedience is pain, suffering, and sorrow beyond "normal" human anguish. For a little humor, I once put in the church bulletin a commentary about tithing: "People say that money *flies*, money *talks*, and money *walks*. If we can teach our money to do all of that, we can teach it to *tithe!*"

Downsizing has become a new word both in today's business world and in the lives of many who are moving into their golden years. The baby boomers are getting older. The 55-plus communities are a rapidly growing real estate phenomenon. Folks want to live freer, simpler lives—one reason among others for downsizing. Such a transition has been my recent experience. To my horror, instead of one day with three movers and five friendly helpers, it still took me three full days to empty the house a week after the estate sale was completed.

The experience pushed me to my knees to beg forgiveness for too often getting what I wanted instead of wanting what I already had. From the clothes closets to the kitchen cabinets to the memorabilia area in the garage, God had lavished my life with treasures great and small. A sense of giving on a brand-new scale has been awakened in my soul, as I seek to return a bit more of the love that has been deepened and intensified in my heart.

Throughout too much of life, I have looked at what I didn't have and needed to get. Now I see clearer what I do have and, consequently, need to give. Such was and is, I believe, the journey of becoming a *certain woman called by Christ.*

Reflections

Many say that there are only two kinds of people in the world: givers and takers. In which ways does your salvation experience prompt you to support or give to the cause of the kingdom?

On what do you believe giving in the church is based? On what do you base your church contributions?

A healthy relationship with the Lord changes not only our living but also changes our giving. Reflect on that statement and mentally track your giving for the past year. What conviction from the Holy Spirit do you experience?

*P*rayer

4

certain women
*are trimmed
of excesses*

My MOM WAS A GREAT SEAMSTRESS WHO INSPIRED ME TO LEARN TO sew at an early age. One of the first steps was to trim the pattern before placing it on the fabric to be cut. All patterns came from the manufacturer with a three-quarters-of-an-inch to one-and-a-half-inch border beyond the cutting line. Often, I would see Mom sitting in her easy chair a day or two before she planned to launch a new sewing project. A pile of pattern trimmings at her feet, she prepared the pattern for its primary use—to guide the cutting of the fabric in the shaping of the garment.

Likewise, it seems that most of these *certain women* had excesses trimmed away from their lives to better shape them for ministry and prepare them for the journey—temporal and eternal. Jesus trimmed devils from some and diseases from others. He accomplished whatever else needed to be trimmed before the "pattern" was laid on the cloth of discipleship. The cutting away of excesses can be painful at times because, as *certain women*, we do not always perceive what we *don't* need in order to become more effective servants of the Most High God.

Many years ago, I lived in Sweinfurt, Germany, with my husband, who was in the military. The Protestant Women of the

Chapel (PWOC) planned a conference and Corrie Ten Boom was to be the featured speaker. I looked forward to attending the conference just a couple of hours away along with other ladies from Sweinfurt. We wanted to meet this historic woman who had stood up to and prayed for the Nazis who had held her along with Jews in concentration camps in World War II.

When I awoke the morning of the conference, I had already decided not to smoke a cigarette before leaving home. (Reflecting on that moment, I'm more amazed at that decision in hindsight than in the foresight of my planning for that day.) How strongly the Holy Spirit was preparing for the insight that was on the way. Had I smoked that day, it may have predisposed me to put off the advice I would receive. Beyond that recollection, it was an ordinary day.

Wrestling with aspects of my own spiritual growth and Christian convictions, I had entertained the idea of giving up smoking cigarettes. I had done just that for a couple of Lenten seasons in years past, with every intention of smoking again once Lent was over. However, this time was different. Something more permanent was not only tugging at my heart but also looming on the horizon. All of the warnings about smoking being hazardous to one's health had not become a major public issue at that time. However, any reasonable person knew that God created the human body to breathe and not to smoke and the latter interfered with the former.

Once at the conference, I decided that when Corrie Ten Boom finished speaking that morning, I would make my way to her to ask one question. I could not tell you today what she spoke about because, throughout her speech, my mind was on that question and the changes in my life that could potentially take place.

When I asked her what she thought about smoking, she looked at me with a most tender and loving expression, and then said to me, "My child I do not think that God wants us to be tied to anything." It was one of the most profound moments in my life and Christian pilgrimage because she did not choose to reprimand

> Jesus breaks the power of debilitating behaviors in your life.

me for a bad habit. Neither did she upbraid me with any sense of judgment. Instead, she allowed God to set me free—to *trim me of my excesses*—to shed from my life a debilitating habit and an emotional crutch. She became the conduit of deliverance for me. I *saw* Corrie Ten Boom. I *heard* Corrie Ten Boom's words. I *was touching* Corrie Ten Boom's hand. But what truly resonated in my soul were the voice of God and His power releasing me from a wearisome, destructive habit.

Although I never saw her again in person, reading her books and news stories about her, I followed her ministry as she came to the US and continued to traverse the globe to the glory of God. God had brought her from atheist to believer to evangelist to proclaimer. In my mind, Corrie was a *certain woman* within recent Christian history because she gave to the ministry of Christ out of her own resources and, amazingly, never felt the need of a religious title or designation.

Many knew her name, but the individual lives she personally touched—as softly as she had whispered those shackle-breaking words into my ear, heart, and soul—live as a testimony to the transforming power God allowed to reside within and to flow through the life of a little lady named Corrie Ten Boom.

they have new patterns

I could go on from that day to declare to others what it felt like to experience the power of the living Christ. This was no longer a power I read about or simply saw demonstrated in the lives of other believers; His power had actively demonstrated its might in me — taken away *any desire* for a cigarette. It has now been nearly 40 years, and never has that desire returned.

When Jesus breaks the power of debilitating behaviors in your life and trims away the excesses, it is far more than discipline; it is His power that is unleashed in your life against excesses that no demon can ever reinstitute.

Being trimmed of that excess freed me to minister more greatly and contributed greater longevity and quality of health to my life. This is one more example of how God reaches into one's life, most often through a powerful believer who becomes "the scissors" that will trim away the excesses from a life He wants to use. It is a process of freeing the believer unto a greater work, a more profound level of living, and a simpler way of life.

Often, for vacations, we tend to overly pack our belongings, often afraid not to take excessive amounts of items along "just in case." While spiritually, the "baggage" is not overstuffed suitcases that detract from the ease and enjoyment of a journey but baggage we cling to from our yesterdays. This baggage often challenges us in any effort to streamline our lives mentally, emotionally, and especially spiritually. Traveling with Jesus requires one to travel light in the luggage of emotions and light in one's spirit. "Sufficient unto the day is the evil thereof" (Matthew 6:34 KJV).

Imagine *that* power in the life of Mary Magdalene — having been trimmed of *seven* demons! What powerful witness her new life would declare to others as they journeyed to the region of Galilee and even to Magdala, the town from which she hailed that sits on the shores of the Galilee. Now trimmed of her excesses—torments—she could experience a true, abiding, faithful, and deep love. Imagine her in the presence of those "who knew her when," remembering what and how she used to be but seeing her clothed in a new power and strength as she accompanied the Master alongside others who had also experienced His power.

Imagine that power in Joanna, socialite, who had been healed and selected by Jesus to accompany Him and the Twelve on this journey of ministry. "A woman from court society, the wife of a senior royal official, following Jesus! What a sensation! The social middle-class of the Jesus group . . . ," declares author Elizabeth Moltmann-Wendel in *The Women Around Jesus*. Not a blue blood, but a woman poised and socially positioned—comfortable around kings and queens.

Her departure from Herod's court and from the care of her husband, Chuza, was not necessarily permanent nor long-term. What was long-term, as insinuated by Luke, was her ability and commitment to help underwrite the financial needs of Jesus, as evidenced by her healing, wholeness, and especially her liberation. But her presence wasn't only about her money and the financial underwriting. Her life, too, had been radically transformed by the touch, power, and call of the Living Savior! She, too, had been trimmed of her excesses.

Joanna is a special joy to me because she represents the kind of woman who has everything and outwardly needs nothing. She had position, power, and personal possessions, along with a prominent family. Certainly she would have been envied and enviable as she represented having it all and having it all together. However, she reminds me of a family I saw on *Oprah* who lived in a house valued at more than $300,000. They ate take-out, fast-food dinners in separate rooms—portraying an abominable sense of family.

> There had to have been a hole in Joanna's soul as great as the Sea of Galilee.

Likewise, there had to have been a hole in Joanna's soul as great as the Sea of Galilee declaring that all of those material possessions could not fill the deepest desires of the human heart. Like others after her, Joanna laid it all on the line. She's not a *certain woman* because of her socioeconomic status; she's a *certain woman* because she chose to reveal her vulnerability—her need for Jesus the Christ and His power to trim her excesses and bring peace to her very soul in the midst of the abundance that characterized her life.

Imagine Susanna, another *certain woman* whom Luke identifies as one who had also experienced the delivering power of Jesus Christ, and all of the other women who were with Him, trimmed of their issues and healed. These *certain women* were now ready to bear reliable witness to the person, power, and presence of the Lord Jesus Christ.

they have new power

I imagine that personal experience with Jesus's delivering power actually set these *certain woman* apart from most of the Twelve, who had heard folk talk of the power of Jesus and had seen its results, but may not have experienced that power within their very own being as many of the women had. This is, of course, with the exception of Peter, who, during their jaunt to Galilee, was enabled to start walking on water to meet the Master.

In other words, the disciples had witnessed thousands being fed, hundreds being healed, and dozens being delivered, but may not have experienced the healing or deliverance in their physical bodies. Jesus's teachings to them were firsthand, but the greater demonstration of His power may have been only secondhand information for the Twelve according to the Scriptures. Although the Twelve were given authority, *certain women* were privileged with an authentic experience that solidified their knowledge of who Jesus was. This was a distinguishing characteristic. The Twelve had been amazed at His demonstration of power but had not personally experienced it in the same ways.

Within the annals of Christian writ, we have often been told that these women could be with Jesus at the Cross because there was no threat against them. There is sufficient evidence within Scripture itself to correct that assumption. Not only were men killed for identifying with "The Way" but Paul even killed women as well, simply because they professed faith in Jesus Christ. (See Acts 8:3; 22:4.)

Why was it so necessary for Jesus to trim the excesses from the lives of these *certain women?* Although they were healed, delivered, and had demons cast out, this was not only preparation for the short jaunt of ministry from Jerusalem to Galilee and its towns; it was an infusion of His power for the duration of His earthly journey and beyond: His excursion to the Cross, through the tomb, and back—so that the realness of the women observers' faith could feed and nurture others for generations to come.

The 11 remaining disciples did not believe the *certain women* as they announced the proclamation of the angels

(Luke 24:5–7). Yet these women had experienced something profound, something radical. For their faith to be stirred, they needed only to be encouraged to remember what He said to them while He was still in Galilee (v. 6). Luke records that they did remember what He said, and they turned their backs on the tomb and went and "told all these things to the Eleven and to all the others [who were with them]" (Luke 24:8–9).

They could have turned their backs on the world and stayed at an empty tomb to grieve in disbelief. Instead, they turned from an empty tomb to a waiting world, becoming bearers of the greatest news — the good news. These *certain women* were unafraid to tell the news — even the disbelieving Eleven could not dissuade the women nor diminish the fervency of their cry, announcing to the Eleven what had been announced to the women: "He is not here; he has risen!" (Luke 24:6).

How many times has the Lord used something familiar or usual to lead you into the unknown? Their task at the tomb was to further condition His body for a proper burial. This was a normal, familiar task within their culture. But in His omniscience, Jesus knew this time would be different, for their intended preparation of His dead body would instead become preparation for the proclamation of the Living Word.

What John the Baptist had been to the beginning of Jesus's earthly ministry — making straight His paths — so these *certain women* would be to His future ministry; they would carve and create a path along which the gospel would travel for generations to come. As John announced His coming through generations, these *certain women* would announce His power for generations to come.

They may not have been at the Last Supper, but if we are to believe any other aspect of God's Word, we can no less believe that who was at the tomb for this miraculous unveiling was no accident of gender, casual circumstance, or simply normal cultural operation. Rather, it was an aspect of a divine plan to launch this second phase of the ministry of Jesus to the first line of defense of the faith—a faith that was already resident in these *certain women*. They had journeyed with Him. They were not upstarts in proclaiming what He had done for them nor in announcing who He was!

they have new purpose

Confirming their messenger status, these *certain women* were told to tell the apostles that Jesus would meet them in Galilee. The apostles received that information from no other source. The amazement that the women had reported correctly—"disturbed us profoundly"—fills the commentary on the road to Emmaus (Luke 24:22), according to Phillips's New Testament in Modern English). Just as amazing is their concluding statement that, "Some of our people went straight off to the tomb and found things just as the women had described them—but they didn't see him!" (Phillips). Jesus Himself then queried them about their "failing to understand and being slow to believe" (v. 25 Phillips). Jesus never ridiculed, diminished, or cajoled the *certain women* who had proclaimed the timeless, divine message of the gospel: "*He is not here; he is risen*" (Luke 24:6).

Mary's thoughts about someone having stolen Jesus out of the tomb is not a contradiction of her faith. Quite the contrary. Mary Magdalene knew if Jesus had come out of that cave under divine power, He would have been in touch with His followers—the ones who walked with Him in life—immediately. She did not realize that He had a surprise waiting for her only. *"Mary!"* He would call her by name, and she would recognize His voice!

So much must have stirred within her behind those tears. Here is a *certain woman* who had been subjected and objected to, but I imagine this moment felt more like rejection—and it was too much for her to bear. She knew the plan. She understood what the Father intended. She had learned well and had deeply believed. Therefore, she could not fathom Jesus departing without letting her (and others) see His glory beyond the degrading death He had suffered and know His power in overcoming death, hell, and the grave. She knew that He knew she had to see Him one last time. Only He knew how important that was to her. And her descriptive cry out to the disciples was, "I have seen the Lord!" (John 20:18).

It was not because of any particular or peculiar relationship she had individually with Jesus, but she knew His love for the apostles, other disciples, as well as those *certain women*. She didn't need to see Him beyond the grave in order to believe. Quite the contrary: she had to see Him because she *already* so deeply believed.

The gift of His presence was going to give her and the others the power to wait on the Holy Spirit, who would bring the power for them to become God's gift to the entire world. His love had so gripped their souls and removed their excesses that she and the others had no other choice but to continue the journey beyond their time in Galilee—to the Cross, the grave, the Resurrection, and beyond! Those whom Mark may seem to have shut up and shut down after the encounter at the grave, Luke liberated, allowing them in his account of the gospel to be faithful to what Jesus had told them to do.

What was it in Jesus that made women act stronger than the apostles in following in the face of His death? I'm not one who attempts to (and we don't need to) pit men against women in the church today because God is still looking for His creation to love Him with our heart, mind, soul, and strength! Love nurtures. Power manipulates. Love fosters an understanding that power empties out and cannot grasp. Love holds fast through the trials and tribulations and remains faithful while power exchanges one unsuspecting "victim" for another out of a greater loyalty to self.

These women, having been *trimmed of their excesses,* which tend to obliterate some spiritual realities, operated from a nothing-to-lose perspective. Not because they weren't afraid or didn't experience a sense of threat; rather, because the One they loved had given them everything they would ever need. They *had no need* to turn away from Him in His hour of need, for they had somehow understood that what He was doing, He was doing for them. And this made them courageous.

I've had the beautiful privilege of hosting two courageous civil rights giants in my home: one, an African-American; and the other, a native of India, a grandson of "the great one," Mahatma Gandhi. They were in a dialogue about courage before a private audience of about 40 people. Each had literally ushered in great change within their respective countries.

We were mesmerized by their recounting of the objective historical events and their subjective participation and experience in such events. Each was asked about being "so courageous" during such tumultuous times. True to self and historical precedents, they responded that the last thing they felt was courage.

Admired for their courage, the two are: Oliver W. Hill, a lawyer who argued the *Brown vs. Board of Education* case before the Supreme Court, and Rajmohan Gandhi, who joined in the Salt March as a lad to help free his country from British rule. These men realized the world looked on them as men of great courage. They shared that in the throes of the moment, a deep inner conviction simply would let them do no less. Human beings when reduced to their deepest "love" can do no less. Fright flees! The merely rational is not reliable! Love holds fast!

A love so rich, so profound, so powerful that no material wealth could compare, no philosophy or other religion could stand up to, and no other power could threaten, is what was left in these *certain women*. They had been trimmed of their excesses, filled with this divine love, and infused with the courage to face any foe or adversary, all in the name of Jesus, who called them to journey with Him to Galilee and beyond.

eflections

What behaviors seem to hinder or hurt your life more than help? What are your excesses?

How can you streamline your life to enlarge your capacities, increase your quality devotional time, and spiritually enrich your life to the glory of God?

rayer

certain women
are whole women

WHAT ACCOMPANIES THE LORD'S HEALING? WHAT ARE THE RESULTS of His healing touch? What differences do we perceive in our lives? What changes do we encounter? The Lord's healing power always has a residual effect! As His Word never returns to Him void, so His touch upon our lives is not without effect or impact. These *certain women* were healed, having experienced God's healing touch directly and individually within their own bodies—and to what glorious effect.

Jesus Christ's touch of grace and mercy heals our spiritual brokenness, launches us to new levels of wholeness, and further opens our eyes to His greater purpose for us. Often we don't realize how broken we have become. In response to pain and hurt, we tuck away bits and pieces of ourselves for self-preservation, gradually losing more of who we are. We train ourselves to function almost robotically in our days, trying to make it from moment to moment, simply existing until a better day comes along. Jesus's touch will heal any and all of our diseases and virtually recreate us if we let Him. Through His power, we can capture our better selves—lost in oceans of hurt and pain as life's rip currents pull us under and wash over us.

Luke's *certain women* each knew the impact and effect of the Master's touch. Now, as they walked the journey with Him and with one another, they were able to allow, in the words of Abraham Lincoln, "the better angels of their nature" to emerge. They were able to release and shed the hard outer core of their personalities that had developed along the corridors of pain they had experienced.

Luke recorded no complaints that they had; revealed no victims' cries from their lips. I believe Luke knew that we would grasp from these *certain women* a sense of their renewal as they set out on a new journey with the Lord, a journey unlike any other. Whom Jesus healed, He made whole. Whom Jesus heals, He makes whole. That's been my experience.

Much of life had rendered me broken in many ways. That sense of brokenness had a hardening effect on my personality. Some years ago, I barely recognized myself in some circumstances. Oh, what moments of reflection were brought on when I couldn't *believe* some of my hardened words or behaviors toward others. The Lord's Spirit warned me that others to whom I related daily had tender hearts, and I needed to be careful how I spoke with them. That awakening moment literally buckled my knees in prayer because I saw a different image of myself in those gentle words. The healing balm also had ushered in a softening of my spirit and greater peace that began to reflect a better me through my personality. His touch had not only healed. His touch had made me whole again.

Each of us enters this world blessed with untold possibilities, gifts, and capacities endowed by our Creator. Over the course of our existence, each of those attributes encounters untold experiences that begin to shape our personalities, lives, and even, to some degree, our destinies. All human beings, but women especially, have the potential of losing themselves in the varied roles they may play in life.

freed to wholeness

At any given moment, almost as a trumpeter depresses the valves on a trumpet to play notes to a song, so women often depress aspects of themselves in efforts to present the best "music" possible out of their lives. When the mommy valves are depressed on the instrument of our lives, the wife notes are not played and vice versa. When the friend notes need to be played, it probably is not the time for us to play a professional note out of our working lives. How multifaceted we are, and sometimes that can work to our detriment.

How do we create the more harmonious tones and tunes out of this "instrument" we call life, particularly as believing women? How do we meet, maximize, or choose to even circumvent the many expectations leveled at us within our daily encounters with others? To what degree are we religiously or spiritually obligated to meet the reasonable expectations of others? How do we reach out to others without reaching too far, so as to distort who we really are? Perhaps to a detrimental degree, believing women tend to be afflicted with the compulsion of trying to be all things to all people — or at least too many things to too many people!

Before Jesus invited *certain women* to join Him on His journey, He freed them from debilitating states of being that would hinder them from being the quality of whole, focused, committed persons He needed on the journey. He saved them. He delivered them. He healed them. He set them free of demonic influences. Besetting sins, devilish ways, and immature behaviors would have been a few of the ways from which Jesus delivered *certain women*. They could not walk the journey with Him in the status in which they previously existed, and He did not have time to await their evolving "perfection." He had compassion on them. He wanted them to be at their best, so delivering them from detractions and distractions was His choice. Infusing their lives with the quality of freedom and the wisdom and spiritual strength to not misappropriate such freedom was a precious gift to these *certain women* in the moment. In His timely deliverance, I believe Jesus reset the hands on the clock of their human development!

In His touch was the power to change their lives.

When I contemplate how long it has taken me to arrive at certain learning, ways of being, and changes in behaviors, I would know that, in the first century, Jesus could not have waited that long for these *certain women* to arrive at or grow into the women they were created and ordained by God to be. I would imagine that He cut through the experiences that would hurt and harden them and bestowed an abundance of experiences that would soften and polish them, so that they could encounter souls of all kinds in the promulgation of the gospel. In His touch was the power to change their lives.

Jesus "grew them up" quickly in the threefold demonstration of His power over their lives: deliverance, healing, and freedom from all kinds of demonic influence. As the Word is wielded, according to Hebrews 4:12 (KJV), as a two-edged sword, so the power of Jesus must have not only cut asunder behaviors that were not needed, but also added into their lives qualities better fitting to the ministry of which they were a part. They became strong. They became focused. They became committed from the moment Jesus laid His hands upon their lives. The insights Luke shares about their lives are minimal in characterization but mighty in profound and descriptive ways. They are modest in detail but majestic in implication!

I recall the very moment when I cried out to the Lord to send into my life someone who truly loved me. I had been divorced. My mother had died. My sister had died. My father had remarried and moved. My fiancé had broken off the engagement. It seemed I had many friends, but one particular friend had become distant. I cried out to the Lord, "Lord, send me somebody who loves me!"

I could see myself becoming something that I didn't like because of such losses. While I hoped for a husband, God returned my father into my daily life because his wife was confined to a nursing home. What initially seemed a new set of responsibilities was soon revealed as the answer to my prayer: here was someone who loved me so totally, in such godly ways, that I am yet amazed. Such love is the essence of the healing Jesus Christ ushers into our lives, raising us to new levels of health, happiness, and wholeness. *Certain women* are not automatically whole. We experience a greater sense of wholeness as we walk with the Lord, and the effects gradually appear. He frees us from our demons.

delivered to develop

In this day and age, we don't like to think of ourselves as *having demons*. That thought seems to belong to an entirely different era. Though we fully recognize there is evil in the world, we have found many other ways to categorize it. What they called "demons" in that day we don't necessarily categorize as demons today. These certain "sistahs" had lots of issues. We grimace at seven demons but fail to acknowledge that we each have at least two or three with which we ourselves struggle.

Now, I have no illegal addictions, but I am definitely addicted to political discussions on TV and abnormally keeping up with shifting political winds. This causes me to watch too much TV and even spend time responding to those media "talking heads" on topics, often of little significance. Comfort food is another addiction. Instead of eating food that is simply nourishing and filling, I've got to go beyond enjoying the meal to "lovin' it" if I'm going to take my time to either prepare or eat it at all. The first demon steals my time and attention, while the second demon steals my health. Whatever our demons might be today, each believer struggles in and through her or his faith to become more free — perhaps one demon at a time.

Jesus had to cast the demons out of Mary Magdalene. He had to diminish demonic influences so that He would become the dominating influence in her life. Demons could afflict and influence people in various ways, but the end result was always to diminish the person from whom or what God originally and continuously intended for that person to become.

Demons, biblically speaking, could operate on either a physical or spiritual level. For example, with a spirit of bitterness, demons could so sour one's relationships with others that they would lose all positive influence in the lives of those into whom they should have been able to speak a word for the Lord!

Believers tend to get lost in the subject matter of demonic possession, forgetting that Satan is not after them or the person but fighting against every good thing God wants to do in the life of that person! Though Satan is not omniscient like God — knowing all things — he certainly knows us fairly well, from our strengths to our weaknesses. He had captured Mary Magdalene in seven areas of her life. Scriptures do not disclose any substantive description.

No matter the number of demons that may have possessed her, she was evidently fully functioning as a human being and still capable of making normal decisions, even deeply spiritual ones, such as responding to the call of the Lord Jesus Christ.

Possession is thought of as an influence and/or a manipulation of the human individual by an outside evil source. Mary was under Satan's influence in several areas of her life and was manipulated perhaps through some temptations to which she did not possess the strength to turn away.

Some have even wondered whether any believer can be demon possessed, and I have opted for the following explanation. Having perused literature over the years, I have come to realize that there is a distinction in demonic *oppression* and demonic *possession*. I believe that when Jesus Christ is accepted by any person who might be in the throes of demonic possession that Jesus breaks that bondage and delivers that believer into His possession! From that moment throughout the rest of the believer's life, she or he cannot ever again be possessed but can be used by Satan in ways leading to demonic oppression—but not possession. No Christian can belong to Satan. We are bought and paid for by Jesus Christ and His blood, claimed and maintained by the blessed Holy Spirit, and cannot belong to any other power that attempts to supplant the ownership of the Risen Christ!

We are bought and paid for by Jesus Christ and His blood, claimed and maintained by the blessed Holy Spirit.

Peter warns all believers about demons: "Be sober, be vigilant; because your adversary the devil, as a roaring lion, walketh about, seeking whom he may devour" (1 Peter 5:8 KJV). That, too, would speak to oppression rather than possession as some might think. Timothy S. Morton puts this in perspective in his book *Christians and Demon Possession: Can A Christian Be Demon Possessed?*

> *Even if demon possession of a Christian is not possible, that, in itself, is of little consolation. Until death or the rapture the ONLY part of a believer that is secure and beyond harm is his redeemed soul. **Everything else he has can be lost or destroyed** and is subject to satanic control or manipulation. Satan can take or destroy a Christian's **health, body, spouse, children, money, job, testimony, church, Bible, rewards, peace, contentment, safety, security, and even his mind without possessing him!*** (Emphasis added)

He characterizes demonic oppression as influencing people from the outside in; and demonic possession as influencing or dwelling inside and manipulating him or her internally. Morton concludes, "Practically all will agree Satan has access to every believer *from the outside* to tempt and appeal to self-will, in an effort to make him or her useless for the Lord," drawing the readers' attention to both James 4:7 and to Ephesians 4:27: "to resist the devil" and "do not give the devil a foothold."

broken vessels for His glory

Part and parcel to this wholeness Jesus gives is honesty. *Certain women* have an honesty about them. They know how empty pretense can be. They have realized they have no need to pretend when the Lord they serve knows them so genuinely and intimately that pretense on any level and in any quadrant of their lives interferes with the power of their lives. They cannot live without His power. *Certain women* seek in this honesty to be whole not only in the manifestation of their lives, but as well in their perception of themselves. They don't mind acknowledging what is *real* in themselves if it will bring glory to Him!

They cannot live compartmentalized lives — separate sets of criteria for separate roles or facets of their lives. Instead they choose to know themselves, warts and all, and fix who they are, to be authentic. Culture has taught us to "fix our faces" in thousands of ways to meet the world! Culture has taught us that we should look certain ways as wives, mothers, professionals; certain ways *ad infinitum*. Culture has at times scathingly criticized women who might have "found" themselves and who relate to anyone and everyone out of that healed place that no longer allows a divided self, but fosters wholeness. That place is often the saving relationship with Jesus Christ, whose discontent with our brokenness led Him all the way to the Cross.

What are the facets of womanhood? The list is exhaustive and even contradictory, yet fun to contemplate.

All human beings are complex to some degree or another. It is suggested by most psychologists that men would tend to be more predictable and women far less so. Therefore, not only from personal experience but also from scientific literature over recent decades, it is strongly suggested that we women folk are significantly more complex than we realize or let on. Some would cringe at that reality and others would do flips of joy over its declaration. I'm in the latter category. Have you realized how complex you are, or are your complexities still buried under the tons of expectations and limitations of others?

What are we to take from this? What are we to learn from the predeliverance, prehealed days of these *certain women*? What is their brokenness showing us? God doesn't call perfect people into His ministry! He taps folk whose lives can become mirrors of His grace, reflecting His power to dramatically transform them from who they were to who He wants them to be and become. God uses broken things and broken people who then, by His power, become whole. As Vance Havner declares in the *Chistian Reader*, "God uses broken things: broken soil to produce a crop, broken clouds to give rain, broken grain to give bread, broken bread to give strength." It was the broken alabaster box that gave forth perfume. It was Peter, weeping bitterly, who returned to serve the Christ with greater power than ever.

We women, perhaps more than men, take on a victim mentality more readily. Doing so, we allow the past to sink us into depression in the present and overcast our tomorrows with clouded skies. Then "doom and gloom" becomes our perspective on life. Linda Mercadante raises the poignant question in her writing, "Winners or Whiners? Victims Caught Between Anguish and Grace," *Journal of Theology*:

> But, first, what is a victim? ... Victims are persons caught in some form of traumatic unfairness, which is life-changing and disempowering. ... Victims are not only unjustly hurt; they have been rendered powerless by the attack, even if only for a short time. Both internal and external resources have been inadequate.
>
> In victimization, self-protection fails and outside intervention is unavailable or ineffectual ... They may be forced, manipulated or lured, but in every case, their agency

is stolen, paralyzed, or considerably diminished ... their
hope and human vulnerability used against them.

How does a victim become whole? How does a woman, after she has been delivered by the Lord, get on with her life and rise to a new level of being? Mercadante suggests:

> *Whether one grows stronger at the weak places, or lives*
> *forever in bondage to their anguish is the most crucial*
> *issue at stake. Often victims need a sense that they have*
> *been heard, their abandonment has been reversed, and*
> *that justice in some measure has been done before the*
> *hold of anguish can be loosened. This cannot be done*
> *alone, but only by a community of co-sufferers, whether*
> *they share the experience by empathy or similarity.*

The author cites S. Paul Schilling, who explains that the root of our English word *anguish* arises out of the Latin word *angustus*, meaning narrow. "The word ... conveys the feeling of being radically constrained, forced into narrow confines ... but even this cannot prevent God's grace from squeezing in around the cracks."

Jesus continuously enlarges our options. From His biblical ministry until this very moment, Jesus does not allow us to be so constrained, restricted, and limited to such narrow confines in life. Jesus knows how to lift us up and raise us to new levels of life and service! Grace, indeed, does squeeze in around the cracked places of our lives, becoming for us not only our healing balm but potentially the spiritual glue that will put us back together again and make us whole.

This insight helps us to see how critical to the success of Jesus's ministry was the decision to include *certain women* and not just a token woman to "decorate" the group of 12 male disciples. Here is where Luke demonstrates not only a personal need for community for all humans but particularly a church need if we are going to accomplish all that Jesus requires. A brand-new, sustainable, and enduring sense of community must begin to more adequately define the church as we know it in the twenty-first century.

Too many relationships in the church are broken. Too many believers in the church range from just hurting to being outright devastated by other believers' behaviors. Too many seekers become disillusioned with the pious pretense they unearth in the church. When there is such great power available to every believer to become whole and filled with grace and love, we need to reexamine why we as hurting people continue to hurt people. Many folk monitor the statistics of new members who walk the aisles and join a local church community; more folk have begun to notice that we (as church leaders) have become experts at bringing folk into the church but still have a long way to go in spiritually "growing up" those we bring in.

Therein is the issue of wholeness. Wholeness does not equate with perfection. It simply suggests a deeper, healed, growing, vibrant, forgiven-and-forgiving, abiding relationship with the Risen Lord. Like the question Jesus posed to the man who had laid by the pool of Bethesda for 30 years, "Wilt thou be made whole?" (John 5:6 KJV) The emphasis of the Lord was upon the man's desire, his will, his intention. Jesus knows that the power is available to us if only we desire to tap into it. So it is today for every believer. In our brokenness, it's time we allowed that question to reverberate within the confines of our very souls: *Do you want to be made whole?* The grace is ours, the love it takes, and the power needed are yours for the asking.

eflections

Men and women have been taught to look for their "other half," neglecting to become the whole persons that God created them to be. Are you feeling diminished in any way in light of that teaching?

Knowing that God did not make half human beings, which part of yourself have you hidden from God? Self? Others? Or which part have you simply neglected to develop?

Which part of your life—personality, talents, abilities, interests, or spirit—yet challenges you towards fuller exploration?

Do you have enough love in your life to become whole? What are the sources?

*P*rayer

certain women
are not self-limiting

WHAT DOES IT MEAN TO GLORIFY GOD? MOST OF US KNOW THE WORD *glorify* well if it's in worship or relative to our worship experience, particularly when singing the doxology. But from the mundane to the highly exalted experiences of our lives, what does it mean for us to glorify God? In the kitchen, in the living room, in the den, in the bedroom, on the front porch, or chilling on the deck, what does it mean for us to glorify Him? Simultaneously it means giving our best, keeping Him foremost in our minds, and willingly becoming vehicles of blessings in the lives of others. Most importantly, it means intentionally developing a deeper, more intimate relationship with the Lord in and through His Word. Too many believers are *Word-starved*, which is a sad state because there's so much in the Word that will strengthen our weary souls and renew the tattered edges of our Christian witness.

These *certain women* demonstrate that our ability to glorify God finds its first expression in service to His Son, Jesus Christ, and its next expression comes in allowing the rest of life to be shaped by, in, and through that service. Once in His path, trimmed of excess and made whole, the *certain women* became devoted servants of the gospel ministry of Jesus Christ. His work was primary. The balance of their lives became a blessed secondary experience to their evangelistically focused walk with

God wants each of us to experience His love, grace, and mercy richly.

Jesus. The essence of their experience with Him became the source for substance in the rest of their lives.

What they had experienced with Him also became the substance of their lives when He was no longer with them. The love He poured into their lives while they were together became the source out of which they learned how to love others. I would imagine that the love, genuine care of the Good Shepherd, and hospitality Jesus poured into their lives became the water that primed the pump on the day of Pentecost and thereafter as they poured into each others' lives provision and possessions so that, according to Acts 2:44, they were "together and had everything in common." Being true to *that* love brought glory to God whether a crowd saw its display or not. Why? Because God continued the unfettered, unbroken, unhindered love that He initially poured into their lives through Christ.

God wants each of us to experience His love, grace, and mercy richly, as He did the *certain women* and each person He has created. Our prayer should be that others experience the joy of the Lord that comes by being *conduits* of such blessed love that the Bible tell us about. "The grace of our Lord was poured out on me abundantly, along with the faith and love that are in Christ Jesus" (1 Timothy 1:14). His love, so marvelous and life affirming, bears power to inspire, deliver, and direct one's life.

What I have received from God is not what I pray that others will also receive directly from God—though they may, and it's wonderful if they do. However, God has us so deeply connected as human beings that we don't need to wait for God to bless others as He has blessed us. But as we seek to glorify God, we *become* the blessing. The abundant call of God to "love one another" in Scripture is sufficient evidence to allow what God has given each of us to become the very source that fuels, energizes, and provides what we pour into the lives of others. That unbroken continuum of both qualities and behaviors of human beings that reflect the goodness of God is what redounds to the glory of God.

Day by day, life reveals to us who we are as people, as believers, as well as who we are not. We are, and more greatly become, the sum of our decisions, the collection of our choices that we have made in varied circumstances. These *certain women* were not perfect and this author has no intent to make them angelic or to use the rag of history to wipe away any negative realities. They are rightfully lauded as having been chosen by the Christ to share in His earthly ministry. However, Jesus called humans in their raw, unpolished, spiritually diminished states because He knew what power He would make available to them.

As they set out on the journey with Him, certainly there would have been some naysayers criticizing their decisions to follow this itinerant preacher. Certainly there would have been at least some wonder: *What am I getting myself into?* There would have been some self-doubt as well as aspersions of doubt cast by others. However, these women mounted their courage, surmounted the verbal obstacles, and chose not to limit themselves to what they already knew and had experienced in life before Jesus. Once they encountered Him and His power poured into their lives, no longer could life ever be the same. They loosed their mental, emotional, and spiritual shackles and set off in newfound freedom to become the women God wanted and the person Jesus was calling each of them to be.

Jesus did not expect Joanna to become Mary any more than He wanted Peter to become John! They were very different people who had already walked very different paths in life. Jesus was not out to make them cookie-cutter princesses but to empower them to take the limits off of their own imaginations as to who they were and were yet to become. Jesus needed them in their uniqueness. He welcomed their idiosyncrasies. He was not afraid of their different personalities. He knew that, in Him, He could hold together their differences, and as they remained faithful with and in Him, He could indeed create something bold and beautiful in and through them (Colossians 1:17).

Limiting oneself is limiting the power of God! These women had seen and experienced the power of God at its greatest within their divine/human encounter. They were not about to lose this opportunity by denying the power that had already changed their lives. They could still recognize their faults but, more importantly, when Jesus came into their lives, they perceived their greater possibilities. Not limited by gender or by culture, they gladly marched with Him from town to town to help set other women free from historic and religious shackles as they, too, faced and responded to a new spiritual force in their midst.

from the mountaintop to the valley

When we know that we *belong* to God, it is far easier to reflect the essence of who He is in us and be integrated deeply into His life. Paul declares "in him we live and move and have our being" (Acts 17:28).

Too often, we have wonderful spiritual experiences with the Lord in worship through blessed singing and anointed preaching;

we even hear the truth of God's Word proclaimed one to another, giving Him glory; then, one or two steps outside of the sanctuary, we revert to cultural behaviors few of which, if any, bring glory to God. The mountaintop experience of the transfiguration becomes twisted into an almost so-called Las Vegas mentality: *What happened up there stays up there.* All that power, all that revelation, and all that glorious experience were never meant to be limited to self on the mountaintop.

> *Peter and his companions were very sleepy, but when they became fully awake, they saw his glory and the two men standing with him. As the men were leaving Jesus, Peter said to him, "Master, it is good for us to be here. Let us put up three shelters—one for you, one for Moses and one for Elijah." (He did not know what he was saying.) While he was speaking, a cloud appeared and enveloped them, and they were afraid as they entered the cloud. A voice came from the cloud, saying, "This is my Son, whom I have chosen; listen to him." When the voice had spoken, they found that Jesus was alone. The disciples kept this to themselves, and told no one at that time what they had seen.*
>
> —LUKE 9:32–36

The experience took place there but the essence of that experience was intended to flow down that mountain through those disciples like a mighty rushing stream of God's glory in the form of transformed human beings and their behavior. According to Richard Longenecker in *In God's Presence*, "They in their full identification with him belonged to God and life needed to be oriented from that perspective." To know that Jesus belonged to God and not understand that of themselves as well, given this divine-human relationship they had with Jesus, was to sever that relationship or to render it meaningless and ineffectual.

God had brought the *certain women* followers together into a Master-servant relationship with Jesus—they were to serve Him as Master. They were to follow as He led, and He would teach them true service to others. Having uttered more than 20 "I Am's" throughout the Gospels (most in the Gospel of John), He knew who He was but, at the same time, He would teach them how to transcend one's identity to move into true servanthood. He formed within them a broader, more comprehensive understanding that they were more than *just* daughters, mothers, and wives. Liberation was the order of the day. Not as we perceive it as in protests; rather, as finally removing spoken and unspoken limitations both self-applied as well as those inflicted by other folk, history, religion, and culture. *All* of who they were became serviceable to the Divine and to the thousands He had come to save.

I have spent more than 60 years in church life and have witnessed that this still seems the most difficult personal hurdle to surmount: not to decry the limitations that others place on us but, rather, the limitations we place on ourselves. It doesn't matter how such limitations occur and whether such limitations are woven into our lives through the fabric of our emotions or happen to emerge through the conduit of our spirit. The reality is that such perceived limitations are there.

We allow the limited vision we have for our lives or the minimal confidence we possess relative to our abilities to inflict doubt and afflict faith. We tend to put it all into how we look. In other words, we rationalize that if we *look* successful, then we must *be* successful. At least, we make ourselves feel that way, no matter how temporary that feeling might be.

On the other hand, we often are unable to forget self in service to the gospel. We fail to eliminate many of our self-promoting behaviors. Either way, faith is not served. Too often, the thought pattern is this: *"What am I going to get out of it? How will this benefit me or someone I love or am friends with? Will this endear me to the pastor or some other significant person in the church?"* Jesus seldom looms large in those moments, and faith is used at those times as a manipulative tool to grasp something for self. Love "vaunteth not itself" (1 Corinthians 13:4 KJV).

from limitations to great expectations

As mistress of ceremonies for a fashion show, I found that the host hotel manager refused to provide a podium of any kind, although various rental fees had been paid. I took off running down the steps of the hotel toward the manager's office. I intended to ask, "What is your problem?" as we were rapidly trying to prepare to open the show. I had 3-by-5 cards about the guest models and 3-by-5 cards describing their outfits. *Where will I place all the cards as I read them?* I thought as I headed straight for the manager's office.

A lady who saw me running down the steps—evidently with a scowl on my face—queried, "Sistah, what's wrong?" I hurriedly explained the mean behavior of the manager. Without batting her eye she exclaimed, "Sistah! Just do it!" I was at the fourth step from the bottom of my trek, but that comment spun me around to run back up that flight of stairs. And *I did it—no hindrances! In a moment, every limitation and hindrance was overcome.*

Certain women are not self-limiting, thinking God created them to only become wives and mothers. How beautiful are those roles, but they are just that, and God does not give every female those roles to fulfill. As He may not have given to the Apostle Paul the role of husband or father, neither does God expect each believing woman to fulfill the roles of wife and/or mother within her lifetime. Many women pray for motherhood and to become wives, and only some are granted such opportunities, but not automatically. Of the 182 million women in the US, slightly more than half marry and about 65 percent become mothers. That leaves out a large cadre of women who never marry nor ever become mothers.

So then, what do we have the right and privilege to expect of ourselves? What kind and quality of life can we envision in the absence of becoming wife or entering into motherhood? Who are we if we are never given that image or role as wife or mother? Mary, the Mother of Jesus, was given the privilege of knowing that she had an exceptional role in the kingdom by giving birth to the Son of God. However, she was ultimately content to be "the handmaid of the Lord" (Luke 2:38). Though no clear-cut, isolated, exceptional roles as such are our destiny, we can glean a solid measure of our function as it relates to being effective in the church and the kingdom of our Lord.

Too often we wait and wait and wait, so intensely focused on marrying and becoming mothers that we limit ourselves to minimal tasks within the church and limit our involvement until we can put together those other key pieces of our lives. Such limitations are incomplete visions of who women are and what they can become. We are more than wife. We are more than mother. We are handmaidens of our Lord to serve, and to function in His kingdom according to the gifts and abilities He has placed in us.

We not only limit ourselves in time. We limit ourselves in treasure. We limit ourselves in talent. I love that Nike slogan, "Just Do It!" (for the love of the sport) or, for *certain women*, for the love of the Master! That's a slogan that controls love for the objective and marshals all of our energies to be successful, despite our limitations and the obstacles that will come.

Certain women are not self-limiting, thinking God created them to only become wives and mothers.

Reflections

Think of one time when you have said, "Oh, I could never do that!"

Now reflect on why you chose to limit yourself in that way.

Living one's life in comparison with anyone else's is a denial of God's wisdom and power in who He made you to be: a woman with such beautiful uniqueness. Do you have a comparative heart that says, "I'm less than . . ." or " I'm better than . . ."?

What experiences has God given you to share in your church, community, and spheres of influence in the world?

*P*rayer

certain women
are intergenerational

CERTAIN WOMEN ARE AS MUCH AT HOME WITH WOMEN 20 YEARS younger as they are with women 20 years older than themselves. They give to both, and they receive from both. They realize that chronological age is no certain indicator of spiritual maturity or immaturity. They also realize that the Lord's work needs a level of energy and well-developed capacity as well as a bona fide spiritual level of competence. That makes *certain woman* pivotal in their service to the Savior, gleaning what's needed from whichever directional source—energy or wisdom—He chooses to send. Friendships are important for *certain women*, but friendship does not become the criteria on which they decide who does what in church ministry.

The biblical *certain women* represented a broad spectrum of womanhood, from young girl Mary Magdalene to, I imagine, a mature woman Joanna to, possibly, a 30- to 40-year-old Susanna. Thrown together by virtue of a call into Jesus's ministry, generational differences were awash in their relationships. In today's jargon relative to generations, "hip-hop" would have been side-by-side with "old school."

About 10 years ago, I was on the African isle of Zanzibar, off the northeast coast of the mainland near Tanzania, to glean from an assortment of women some thoughts about issues as well as their needs and personal concerns. We were attempting to single out a few women to invite to an international women's conference. Sitting in the semicircle in front of us were women of various generations; some were quite aged and others were quite young.

After engaging them in conversation for some time, I noticed that only the younger ones were conversing with us visitors. I stopped the proceeding, believing there was either a problem or misunderstanding. Our visiting delegation expressed great concern. How much we wanted each woman to feel a part of this process, to share her own thoughts and comments about issues dear to her. I was struck by our hostesses' response—both the older and younger women. They laughed!

Had our translator communicated incorrectly? Had I committed a social or cultural *faux pas*? On further questioning, the younger women became more sheepish, whereas the older women seemed emboldened—the reverse of their earlier behavior. As they explained, laughter broke out all around and a warm, soft, and gentle spirit that affirmed both the older and younger women pervaded the room. One woman finally jumped up from her seat and declared, "Well, the younger women have the education and know how to speak, but it's the older women who tell us what to say." And they served the ministry of Jesus "out of their own means." The generations had had conversations before our arrival and endeavored to communicate the best of their needs, issues, and concerns by slipping the wisdom of the ages into the "glove" of the younger women's education, in order to share their best efforts and obtain the most appropriate responses to their shared needs.

informing in the church body

So often in the church, we want to do things *for* our youth and young adults rather than *with* them! We too often allow ourselves as more mature women in the faith to become alienated from those who are newer to the faith. How then can such a negative "grounding" of our relationships serve the more positive purpose of building the kingdom of our Lord or the church? It cannot. Therefore, it is incumbent upon *certain women* who are more mature in the faith to find ways to befriend our members in the faith as we build events, programs, the church, and the kingdom together.

Though it's not the *end all*, we also must try to remember the time when we were young and even, perhaps, a little foolish. We must learn to laugh at our own foibles and stumbles along the learning path of life, while recognizing that each woman has something to give to the successive generations. Jesus said to Peter, "When you get yourself straight, turn and strengthen your brother!" (Luke 22:32, author's paraphrase). Jesus was not limiting such instruction to those who were the peers of Peter, but was declaring that when Peter *came to himself*—the self that God had shaped within him—then Peter would have life-changing episodes out of which to share. This sharing would have a profound impact on the lives of the faithful coming behind him.

Women in heaven won't be exclusively gray-haired, church old-timers. Those full of faith across the spectrum of age will fill the courts of the Lord with heartfelt praise. My question is this: how will we praise together *in heaven* if we cannot praise Him together *on earth?* We have been given that capacity not to just reach out and win the lost but to strengthen the found! Too often we focus more on evangelism than discipleship and more on discipleship than Christian community and more on superficial fellowship of eating and banqueting than in the intentional ministry of building spiritual relationships within the church family.

An overemphasis on evangelism has made even a few megachurches become sites for revolving doors relative to their new members. Yes, large numbers come, get acclimated to some degree, stay a little while, and then are gone elsewhere to serve the kingdom into which their faith has placed them. However, discipleship and, most importantly, a sense of integrating people into meaningful community circles within the church contribute best to a vibrant church.

Young people will not automatically *know* how to worship the Lord, but they are in church because they *want* to worship the Lord! We too often criticize and condemn what they wear and what they offer as they have opportunities to present their gifts and talents. Instead, we should come beside them in Christian love to help infuse them with a love for the Master that can reduce their sociocultural influences and raise the spiritual influences in their lives. Criticism and condemnation of any other believer creates anger instead of responsiveness to the love of Christ that should pervade the church.

Certain women reach back, forward, and out to believers of all kind, knowing that each person has much to give and to receive as they walk together in and out of contemporary "cities" and head towards the New Jerusalem! *Certain women* are not intimidated by the exuberance of the youth or the political power of church seniors. It is our faith that validates us; indeed, it is only our faith that matters and out of which comes—what Paul in his letter to Philemon calls—every good thing we have in Jesus Christ.

Such a letter models for us the reality that we do not walk this journey of faith alone. Neither is our experience of faith an empty shell in this life awaiting fulfillment on the other side. No! A thousand times no! Right now, we have every good thing in Christ Jesus our Lord! Paul declares, "I pray that you may be active in sharing your faith, so that you will have a full understanding of every good thing we have in Christ" (Philemon 6).

Paul already had commended Philemon about his "love for all the saints" in verse 5, and certainly meant that without regard to age, stage, or status in life. Because it is in this biblical book, this letter, that he was preparing to send a young runaway slave back to his master along with a couple of other young brothers in the faith. So Paul had a great grasp on sharing the faith across generational lines and allowing that faith to transcend the differences that might arise because of age and past behaviors.

It was such a love that Paul declared had "given [him] great joy and encouragement" and had "refreshed the hearts of the saints" (v. 7) because of its life-giving power and its strength of encouragement. Many youth coming into the church are as Onesimus was, because of what Christ has done in their lives: "Formerly he was useless to you, but now he has become useful" (v. 11). Paul was not sending a strange new member of the church to Philemon but a young man Paul had come to know and love as a son. He was endeared to Paul not only on a spiritual level but also on a

Certain women are not intimidated by the exuberance of the youth or the political power of church seniors. It is our faith that validates us . . . it is only our faith that matters.

practical, familial, human level. It was a rich relationship between an old man facing death and a young man trying to make a life for himself. Moving in opposite directions to some degree, they found commonality in the church and their Christian-based relationship, along the continuum of faith. Both of their lives were enriched.

Notice the contrast: Paul was in chains while loosening the chains that bound a fellow believer. Paul's chains were physical, whereas the chains on Onesimus's life were spiritual and emotional. Technically, Onesimus was a free young man living a long way from his former slave master and a long way from the past he had had in Philemon's household. Paul found some element of divine purpose in Onesimus being Philemon's runaway slave. He stated that the one who was formerly *useless* to Philemon was now *useful* both to Paul and potentially to Philemon. Within this divine vision Paul casts over the life of Onesimus, Paul sees and declares, "Perhaps the reason he was separated from you for a little while was that you might have him back for good—no longer as a slave, but better than a slave, as a dear brother" (v. 15–16).

What a turnaround for a young person of faith! All made possible by those older in the faith, who took the time to be intergenerational. Paul, the older, facilitated the return of a younger fellow into a good relationship with a middle-aged man in the faith and the first-century church. Talk about *intergenerational.* What a model!

linking the younger and older

Many of our young men and women, virtually streaming into some of our churches, need that kind of support and care.

They will open up to those who open up to them. They will walk with those who will walk with them in the faith. They don't need another mama or papa! What they need is a type of Paul, Philemon, Mary Magdalene, Joanna, Susanna, Salome, or another in their lives to help fill 'em up with faith and then share the courage and strength with them to clean up or sever themselves from their past! It will take intergenerational people of faith to accomplish that, not meddling busybodies who gossip about and criticize instead of sharing faith.

Yes, *certain women* are intergenerational. We don't simply teach children in Sunday School, small groups, and Bible studies. We migrate towards young folk who enter our church families and help to encourage and sustain them emotionally as we nurture them spiritually. Visiting their homes and schools for certain events, encouraging them in their life decisions and peer relationships, remembering them on their birthdays and at Christmas are a few ways to begin to step into intergenerational relationships—prayerfully and with parental and pastoral awareness and approval.

In further contemplation, this becomes even more exciting because I've met many an older person whose faith has grown a little weak and thin at times, and that younger person in the faith can come right along and speak a faithful word that is better than a shot of penicillin against the disease of doubt! We need each other across the divides of age and stage in life. And if Jesus is in our midst as He was on the journey with Luke's *certain women*, then each of us will fare far better than we ever could alone.

I have found that we never get too old to be young, nor are we ever too young to be old in the sense of wisdom and knowledge. We are all learners of each other if we truly bestow

> We are all learners of each other if we truly bestow significance on one another. That is the . . . hurdle.

significance on one another. To me, that is the tremendous hurdle we each must "jump" if we are to be intergenerational. If we have difficulty attributing *significance* to those who are not of our age or stage, that makes us counterproductive in the gospel work within which Jesus declared that we (the older ones) m*ust* become as *little children* (Matthew 18:3). He saw the children as having more of what God the Father wanted than whatever the aged might possess.

Schools struggle today with the federal program called "No Child Left Behind." The spirit of NCLB is that no child in public school across this nation will be devoid of the academic experiences that would improve his or her chances at being able to succeed. Translate that sentiment into the need within our churches to care for our children and young people. Too often we have "left them behind," filling them up with practical things and leaving them empty spiritually. We have the resources within our congregations to provide for and train our youth in the mechanics of leadership and to provide the spiritual "smoothies" that will nourish their very lives!

Mary Magdalene, Joanna, and Susanna were free to pour into each other's life the very best of what they knew of themselves: wisdom from life experiences, relational experiences, and faith experiences. In Jesus's presence, would they have quested for any less than the best for each other? They had much to share and much to learn from one another while they learned from the Lord. They had experienced much and their turnaround was profound. They had much to share in areas of real love, transparency, truthfulness, trust, and even finances.

Matthew 12:34 declares, "Out of the overflow of the heart the mouth speaks." Can you imagine these women after they had been healed and delivered as well as had demons cast out of their lives? They had reasons to be glad because, in the process of such transformation, what and who they loved was also changed! So their talk with one another and about one another changed. In their old temperaments, they may have pointed out imperfections in others but in their newfound relationship with Jesus and with one another, they found a new purpose and destiny as they appropriated this new power of God into their lives and especially in their speech.

making certain and SOLID impact

Reflecting on this sense of making relationships "solid" in the church, I considered people I've known. Nothing can ever sever our relationships. We are still at each other's beck and call. I may not have seen them for 40 years or so, but still feel the impact of their faith within my life.

- That *certain* very senior lady taught a Bible study on Romans in 1968–69. I can still hear her voice. Her capacity to pour the great truths of God's Word into us was nothing short of transforming—a miraculous power that continues today.
- *Certain women* in Sunday School encouraged us in how to behave, dress, live, speak, and give reports and poured their faith into us in so many ways across those generational divides.
- *Certain women* fully affirmed and validated us as leaders in the church, no matter our age or stage!

As a result of their lives, an acronym comes to my imagination that simply describes what it means to love: **S**hare **O**ne's **L**ife **I**n **D**eeds! It wasn't what they *said* to us as much as it was what they *did* for us that made the greatest difference.

Recognizing what they have poured into many young lives, I began to wonder what essential matters of the faith would I and do I share with others who are chronologically and spiritually of a different generation. How can I help to make another believer's pilgrimage a bit easier than my own? How can I manage to inspire them with truths and testimonies that will lead them deeper into the Bible? What can I pass on that others have sown into my life to awaken me to more of God's truth—truth that has shaped not just my life but my appetites, preferences, and choices in every area of living? What are the top ten realities of this faith pilgrimage that I would share in every conversation and whenever possible—spiritual and biblical wisdom that have made such a difference in my life? Here are the results of that pondering:

top ten realities

1. **Go to God, not only to church.** We raise generations of the faithful with the orientation that being *in church* is the cornerstone of the spiritual life. Actually, the development of *a personal spiritual relationship* with Jesus Christ is the cornerstone. Out of that relationship, worship and service to the church will be enriched. A prayer life is desperately needed! A church life without a strong prayer life that can stand on its own is religion and not faith. We need to grow up generations in the *faith* of our Lord and Savior Jesus

Christ and not within the religious shell of only *functioning* in the church!

2. **Keep God first.** So many believers declare they do not have time in the mornings (or nights) before work or school for personal devotion. They want to wait to get to their desk to pull out their Bible and meditate for 15 minutes or so before their tasks. Think about it. One would have awakened, showered, coordinated wardrobe, dressed, fixed coffee and breakfast, brushed teeth, found keys/wallet/pocketbook, grabbed briefcase, driven to work or school, and greeted those at work before addressing the Savior! All of that is only if they live *alone.* Children, spouse, parents, and pets? Each would add more to that list of preparation for the day. Note how far down that list God is! How then can we honestly *say* we love the Lord with a SOLID-type love? Putting God first means putting God ahead of anything, everything, and everyone else every day. That's the way to live out our faith — and to live *in* our faith from generation to generation.

3. **Create and sustain a joyous prayer life: discipline alone is drudgery.** Cultivate joyous conversations with the Lord. Too often I have found that many believers imagine they are *praying* when they are *thinking about* the Lord. Reflection and meditation are aspects of prayer but neither is the same as praying. Where God is *in your* life is not where you encounter Him when you're in need or in worship; it's where you place Him in your everyday, ordinary life — first and foremost!

4. **Faith must be nourished by the Word *before* bad things happen.** The work of the Holy Spirit is to walk alongside believers to see what we can't see, do what we can't do, teach what we do not know, and comfort us when we face difficulties.

Can you imagine such a friend walking beside us and not alerting us *before* we stumble or fall? That would not be much of a friend or a comforter! Regularly coming to the Word will feed the believer with the right scriptural nourishment *before* he or she comes upon any difficulty. Situations along life's journey might catch us by surprise, but they don't have to catch us unprepared.

5. **If your faith is not *growing*, it's dead or dying.** Anything living must be fed. I will never forget a TV interview during the 1960s. A fellow from a Black activist group had given his testimony about being "born again" while in exile in Europe. On his return to the US, he shared this in an interview. The interviewer declared, "If he was *born again*, it must have been a still-birth!" Have you ever heard anything so cutting about a believer? Faith that is not nourished continuously by God's Word will be supplanted and diminished by the cares and ways of this world.

6. **Monitor your time wisely to avoid misuse of it.** Time is God-given. Everyone has time—24 hours a day! We just tend to misuse it.

7. **Journal.** Chronicle what God is doing in your life. It's exciting to read what you previously wrote, and that will bring new revelations to you as to what God is seeking to accomplish in your life. God is a God of action! What He is doing is important. Make note of it! Chronicle those actions that will help you best *see* the hand of God moving for you, and *trace* from whence He has brought you!

8. **Never isolate yourself from other believers.** No matter what happens in life, God will always have friends waiting for you at each and every juncture. Having faith is remaining

open to those new possibilities. Do all you can to keep those SOLID relationships.

9. **Face every fear.** Make "fear" your friend. Walk with it. Learn from it. Conquer it. Always know that fear is only meant for you to stop, take notice, reflect, get more information, and grow in faith to trust God more! God has given us the capacity to be afraid not to stymie us but to alert us to danger. Once we reckon with the danger, we should perceive the way, a way forward! Resolve within yourself that fear and faith can never occupy the same space. You can live free of fear and full of faith!

10. **Love.** To love is a choice to do good and to do what is right according to the Word. The choice to love is action, not feeling! It's action in spite of how we might feel towards another. If you want to know the real power of the gospel, choose to love. "Love one another. As I [Jesus] have loved you, so you must love one another" (John 13:34).

The religion that we pass on to other generations of believers is only as good as the faith with which it is filled; without the characteristics of love driving such faith, it becomes "sounding brass, or tinkling cymbals" (1 Corinthians 13:1 KJV). Quest for this wisdom, and then seek every opportunity to pour this faith into other believers' lives.

On Valentine's Day 2000, Gail Sheehy, author of *Passages*, speaking at a luncheon, declared that every girl child born that day had the life expectancy of 100 years! And that, if our daughters were going to live longer, "we should teach them how to live better." In the faith, we each have something of significance to teach one another.

Reflections

What do you give to younger generations beyond your own personal family members?

What do you actively seek to receive from older generations?

We often glean energy, capacities, and spiritual competencies from our interactions and meaningful relationships with people of different age levels. Reflect for a moment on whether these wonderful dynamics enrich your life or conduct.

Prayer

certain women
know what
belongs to God

IT CAN BE A STRUGGLE TO FIND OUT WHAT BELONGS TO GOD. ALL OUR lives, we are told what belongs to everyone *but* God! We struggle in the tension of being too oriented to this world or to heaven, being too carnal or too religious. Few of us find a happy median early in life. It seems to take much living to finally get it and feel at home with what Jesus declared to the Pharisees as an object lesson to His disciples as well: "Give to Caesar what is Caesar's and to God what is God's." It was the result of Jesus's exchange with those leaders of His day. Jesus's very presence and ministry threatened the status quo and each human's orientation to former thinking. Reflect on the Pharisees' exchange with Jesus:

> *Watching for their opportunity, the leaders sent secret agents pretending to be honest men. They tried to get Jesus to say something that could be reported to the Roman governor so he would arrest Jesus.*
>
> *They said, "Teacher, we know that you speak and teach what is right and are not influenced by what others think. You sincerely teach the ways of God. Now tell us — is it right to pay taxes to the Roman government or not?"*

*He saw through their trickery and said, "Show me a
Roman coin. Whose picture and title are stamped on it?"*

"Caesar's," they replied.

*"Well then," he said, "give to Caesar what belongs to him.
But everything that belongs to God must be given to God."*

*So they failed to trap him in the presence of the
people. Instead, they were amazed by his answer, and
they were silenced.*

— LUKE 20:20–26 (NLT)

For years, I brushed my hands together, signifying, "Well, that's
that!" or "Guess He told them!" Pay your taxes, vote, pledge
allegiance, do what you must do to honor "Caesar" and just don't
confuse that with belonging to God! But what belongs to God?
What does God want from me? "I'm just _____ ."
(I'll let you finish this sentence because I had to as well.) You're
far more than just _____ ; and God is waiting for
that just _____ to be turned over to Him to make
more _____ out of it! Blessings beyond belief are
part and parcel to the human-divine process of discerning and
then progressing to being capable of giving to God what belongs
to God. These *certain women* who walked with Jesus *knew* what
belonged to God!

How disappointing it is — having shaken many hands — to
receive a handshake that is limp, extended to you halfheartedly
without sufficient intention or focus. God wants us to love Him
lavishly, not limply. This is the human response closest to how
He has loved us. We do not "love Caesar" (political entities/
governments) lavishly when it's tax time. Perhaps we don't mind
paying taxes, but citizens do it under the penalty of going to jail.

As citizens, we want to see the poor, elderly, and other human needs provided for, but just don't tax us too much! We want paved roads for comfort, traffic lights to help manage traffic, and interstates to ease our travel, but often we warn "Caesar," "Don't take too much." But that's not the attitude with which we render anything to God: our tithes, offerings, concerns, or ourselves. Whether from the admonition or revelation that "God loves a cheerful giver" (2 Corinthians 9:7) or from the example of what is presented in the Gospels as "the widow's mites" offering, God loves and expects us to love Him lavishly (Luke 21:1–3).

Joanna proved she knew what belongs to God as she left not only her personal household to join Jesus on this journey but even the household of Herod the king. With all of its accoutrements, that life could not have kept her in Jerusalem or prevented her from accepting the invitation of the King of kings. We know now that her departure was temporary. Her journeying with Jesus on the dusty roads from Jerusalem to and around the towns of Galilee was also, but did she or any of the disciples know it then? They each had left all to follow the Christ. They loved family and friends, their neighbors and neighborhoods no less. They just loved Jesus more. They realized that to truly belong to anyone or anything else, they must first belong to God. This involved then and often now involves a departure of some kind, but not always. Rather, it's a perspective out of which they had to and we must now live; it's the key to living a healthy, brilliant, multifaceted life according to the will of God; it's seeking Him first, knowing that all these other things shall be added unto you (Matthew 6:33).

These were intelligent women; sensitive, spiritual women; women capable of deep devotion, who took life seriously; women who loved life; women who loved their families. But they loved

God more, and they understood how to bring real order and greater management to their lives and greater benefit to their family members' lives by putting God first as they discerned that family, too, belonged to God. I believe they knew the more they loved God, the greater would be their capacity to love anyone else they were privileged to have in their lives.

counting the cost

I was scheduled to fly to England for a speaking engagement March 16, 2000. Unexpectedly, my sister died on March 15. With only an aged father left to look after the myriad details, did I dare not cancel my journey? I asked God first. When I finally told my father what I believed I had to do, he would not agree to delay the funeral from Saturday until the following Wednesday. I pushed that envelope as far as I could without causing him further anguish. I knew what I had to do. For the next few hours, we were virtually silent with one another. The drive to the funeral home to meet with the funeral director was not only filled with grief from the shock of her death but also was defined by a deep divide over when to bury my father's daughter and my sister. I had said all I could. I had pleaded and prayed. Finally, there were no words left.

We arrived at the funeral home Thursday morning, and the funeral director addressed the service details. Without a further word from me, my father told the funeral director that he wanted her funeral the following Wednesday. To this day, I do not know what convinced him to relinquish his preference of burial time to the need and call of my ministry responsibilities.

Before we arrived at the funeral home, I had made peace

spiritually with my beloved sister who, after I was called into ministry, had always understood my need to be obedient even when it seemed inconvenient. If in her living she fully validated that, I knew that I could do no less in her dying. I loved her deeply, yet I had grown in knowing what belongs to God and could love God lavishly in joyous obedience.

A beloved neighbor, who just happened to be a retired home economist and beauty consultant, offered to take responsibility for my sister's makeup and attire. People around you will often step into the gaps when they, too, know you're only going to do what God has called you to do—that you're only attempting to give back to God what belongs to God, not to escape any normal responsibilities. All I knew was that I had to love God lavishly, even in the throes of my unrelenting grief at having lost my only sister and the anguish of having to leave her "on hold" while I obeyed God's mandate for my life.

I knew what belonged to God: my obedience to His call. In his own private way, my earthly father came to that realization as well. I flew across the Atlantic, experiencing tears that mirrored the ocean beneath us. The sadness was heavy, but the peace in my soul was unmistakable. By the grace of modern technology, I was able to assist our father in taking care of every detail. By phone, I comforted him. He just needed to hear my voice! By computer, I developed the funeral bulletin. By fax, I communicated with the funeral director.

My sister's home-going celebration was far beyond what we imagined it would be. The outpouring of love and sympathy was beyond our capability to measure. Earthly responsibilities can be placed within the proper perspective fairly easily when we learn what belongs to God.

Little girls grow up through their doll-playing; their minds are shaped by and very souls are steeped in the realities of ultimate emotional and physical responsibility for the children they might one day bring into this world. Through the dating years, they learn what will eventually belong to a spouse. They will learn through varying numbers of relationships—as well as from TV, novels, and magazine articles—that a man-woman relationship is virtually all-consuming: all that a woman will be and become belongs to the man she'll choose to marry when and if that time comes.

Education teaches the lesson that you will belong to your job, your profession; your success will depend greatly on your willingness to sacrifice anything and, possibly at times, everything else. Among women particularly, many relationships have suffered as a result of these pressures, which often evolve into the need or expectation to "give it all up"—in the sense of priority if not practicalities—to achieve status or promotion in one's chosen field.

So much mitigates against our ability to know what belongs to God as we grow and mature in the faith! Confusion often reigns. Depression can even wreak havoc spiritually, emotionally, and mentally. Relational losses can pile up before we get a clue about the way in which and the perspective through which we are living our lives with "Caesar," God, and er'body else!

Society teaches the lesson that we are nothing without money, that our value is virtually equal to our bank account or material possessions. More exactly, what we wear seems to define us to a great degree according to society. Society considers us to be little more than what we can own or access: designer pocketbook, upscale car, house in the suburbs, clubs we join, and the schools our children attend.

We're not like the Pharisees: confused and trying to trip up Jesus with a trick question. We need to know, but it's no wonder we might be confused about these questions: What belongs to Caesar? Employer? Husband? Wife? Children? Neighbor? Friend? God? It's no wonder we wrestle with our own sense of being and well-being because all our lives we have been shaped by the voices of culture, tradition, family, and even the voices emerging from our deepest desires. It's no wonder we hardly know ourselves or can barely get to know one another. There are powerful forces warring within our very souls about our true identity in the tension of competing loves and loyalties.

Seeing themselves in His image, many people intuit another voice bouncing off the walls of their spirits, proclaiming that they were meant to be far more than they currently know themselves to be. They experience a chasm between their current identity and that someone that a vision of their future paints or confirms. To say that God is just trying to bless them is to not come close to the reality; to say that they have missed their real purpose in this life is also to misdiagnose their condition. In the midst of all that they are and that they have accomplished, they have believed in the Lord, served the Lord and His church, engaged in missions, done great deeds, achieved reasonable success but know, still, that something is not quite right! Little, if anything, satisfies.

The Pharisees did not have this problem. They were simply trying to derail Jesus's ministry, to get Him arrested or killed so that His "troublemaking" would end. Jesus, in His declaration, not only deals with their immediate question, but makes Himself even more of an enigma than He seemed previously. They are amazed at His wisdom and discernment about their motives.

However, Jesus's words provide us with far more than mere

> The greater problem is coming to terms with that reality: what in us and of us belongs to God?

clarification in a tête-à-tête with the Pharisees, whose inquiry was settled by the very obvious object used in the response that Jesus gave. But this same response by Jesus allows us to affirm not only what belongs to Caesar but also what belongs to God. The coin belonged to Caesar, but the person holding the coin bears no image of Caesar. The image of God has been "stamped" upon each human being and God-like properties have been imprinted within our very souls. There can be no denial of what belongs to God.

Even for the men standing before Jesus in that moment—as well as for *certain women* then and now—the greater problem is coming to terms with that reality: what in us and of us belongs to God? It's exciting to contemplate. Relationships often bring confusion because aspects of ourselves belong to mother, father, sister, brother, husband, children, employer, friend, neighbor, mortgage holder, debtors, *ad infinitum*. How then, do we "collect" ourselves from all these disparate relationships so that we can have the perspective and power to live that life Jesus sought to shape in His disciples and God desires us to have? The Pharisees' exchange with Jesus gives us quite a clue to God's expectation. Jesus's response to the rich young ruler earlier (Luke 18:29–30) helps bring further clarity to the matter:

> *"I tell you the truth," Jesus said to them, "no one who has left home or wife or brothers or parents or children for the sake of the kingdom of God will fail to receive*

many times as much in this age and, in the age to come, eternal life."

—LUKE 18:29–30

I was taken aback by the phrase in Mark's telling of the same incident (10:28–30 KJV) that revealed this leaving all and "hundredfold" return would come "with persecutions"—a real wake-up call! My life finally made sense! There is nothing I have held back, not surrendered, or not left for the Lord in ministry for more than 30 years.

People who leave all to serve Jesus do not love family, home, children, professional fields, and more any less. In fact, they may love those other choices far more. But a greater allegiance to what God expects and wants begins to emerge more prominently in their lives, because looming on the horizon is a true destiny without which they could never endure the regret of not moving in its direction! It's a done deal at that point. They are finally able to see and say, "Lord, I can never be the me you want until I give you the me I now know!" In that moment, they become whole and capable of leaving everything they've ever known, yet not necessarily needing to do that in the moment. It's a matter of living with a more profound perspective of the divine-human relationship than necessarily a change in place or location. Metaphorically, if your life were an arrow, it would finally have a point.

Metaphorically, if your life were an arrow it would finally have a point.

In Scripture, Jehovah God is referred to as the Revealing One. It is awesomely clear to me that the more we allow God to reveal Himself to us, the better also we

certain women called by Christ

get to know ourselves. We begin to see ourselves more clearly for the simple fact that we can then gain a different and better perspective on life than what the world would have shown us previously.

As I reflect on when and what I have left or given up for the sake of Jesus Christ and His kingdom, I'm amazed that many of the problems I experienced become crystal clear. People you have left as well as people you move towards potentially have issue with someone who has the capacity to leave all for the cause of Christ. There is something empowering in you but something threatening to those outside of that experience or decision. Many around you may not understand a love so lavish and may think you've altogether "lost it." Be not dismayed. It takes them a little extra time to arrive at the understanding you have gained about your relationship with the Lord. They intuit your change as their risk and as their threat—that the decisions made will have a negative impact on their lives. To some degree, they might, but the results can actually become far more positive than negative because of the new orientation of "God first."

"And the Twelve were with Him [Jesus] and *certain women*" . . . a few folk who probably knew little about what belonged to God but accepted duties that lay carefully within the boundaries of appropriate religious response. They left all . . . and followed; leaving was not lack of care or loose attachment or shallow affection but a function of the faith that was their response to that godly love they received and from which they could not turn away.

Yes *certain women* know what belongs to God. They can never be content within their own imaginations about their lives nor what culture or tradition alone has taught them. The voice of the

Lord and the power of His Word are just too powerful to ignore or to respond to with minimal effort. God calls for our maximum response, not a response that meets the bare minimums of a practiced religion instead of a gloriously lived life of faith!

The negative side of learning what belongs to God is making a brief review of your life and taking note of the elements that have been rejected by folk around you. Occasionally, when we try to give our time, talents, and treasures to some people, they reject either some element of what we're offering or the whole thing outright. Assessing it "postmortem" helps us to realize that we either gave the wrong thing, the right thing to the wrong person(s), or more of us than they could handle. They often were not equipped to handle what we were offering in our vain attempt to make them receive what should have been given to God by way of the lives, times, and places that He ordained.

Reflections

Folks who don't know God have easily explained the dichotomy between the physical and the spiritual, between body and soul. However, Scripture reveals that God does not see it that way. What in your daily experience do you feel authentically belongs to God?

What do you understand about the process of sanctification?

*P*rayer

certain women
manage their households well

THIS CHAPTER IS NOT ABOUT HOUSE MAKEOVERS OR BECOMING BETTY Crocker. It focuses more on the spiritual than the practical ways of developing good *housekeeping* or, as I choose to state it, *house living* standards that have an impact on every dimension of our lives and every relationship. Often, it's not until we get into the throes of ministry that we discover the tensions ministry can create in our family, marriage, or single life. Learning to manage our households well, whatever the configuration, is key to the level of quality functioning in ministry possible for those who are *certain women* called by Christ.

Managing our households is as foundational to the stability and quality of our lives as managing our ministries are to building God's kingdom. Household and ministry management are mutual dimensions of our obedience to our God and living Lord. Though it may not come easy for some, household management should be a glorious task. It is a substantive part of the witness we proclaim for the world to "see" what God has done in our lives—the first of which was to *speak order* into *chaos!*

On a spiritual basis, of all the *certain women* who accompanied Jesus in His ministry, it was probably Mary Magdalene into whose life the greatest gift of order came. It is probably fair to suggest that Jesus, having cast out seven demons who were wreaking havoc, spoke order into a life rendered virtually unmanageable by destructive power. But with the demonic powers literally cast out, she would have gained capacity and capability to order her life in godly ways. All she needed after that was to learn a few skill sets in managing a household.

Though managing comes much easier when order is spoken into chaos, there are still some skills to be learned from others so that our lives truly can reflect the glory of the Lord. Don't look for a rote method for home management or improvement here. From the *Good Housekeeping* magazine to many others, there are plenty of available practical resources. The surer route is a review of who and what in life is important and to begin living according to those priorities. The closer we get to Christ, the more we want to reflect His life daily. That gives us the power to make the changes we long for—changes that renew, revive, and reshape our lives! The hardest part is beginning.

We would already know that God not only reveals Himself but also His ways and His will for us. The more we find out about God, the better we understand ourselves; the more we read of His Word, the clearer our image in the mirror becomes, and some depth perception of "what I'm all about" in relation to others begins to emerge. In this intimate relationship, we begin to learn more deeply our vast dimensions that have gone untapped and underdeveloped. Were it not for God's revelation about Himself, it would be virtually impossible, I believe, for us to know ourselves and comprehend any dimension of the "why" and "what" of our existence, individually and relationally.

Without such revelation, we would be as abandoned children,

wondering and attempting to uncover our origins. What I have heard in many interviews of abandoned children are these questions: "Why did you give me up?" "Why didn't I matter to you?" "What was so bad about me that you could not put up with me?" or even, "What did I do that made you want to get rid of me?" Such children often look for personal insufficiency. However, Jesus promises not to leave us (John 14:18)! Thank God for truth revealed that no such abandonment of God's creation took place; instead God made special provision for His creation through Jesus Christ, to keep us unto Himself.

What does this have to do with *certain women* managing their households well? It matters not what size or kind of household we might have. What matters is that we are solidly grounded in who we are as people who know God as Creator and Father. When this knowledge is in place, management of what God allows will be of a desired quality and will not serve to negate or diminish how we value ourselves. It is a function of our faith to think well of ourselves because of who we know our God to be! That's a central aspect of becoming mature spiritual adults: securing *who we are* and being comfortable with *what we* are meant to *become*. As *certain women*, we are neither abandoned nor incapable of managing our households well.

experiencing *shalom* at home

Some women lack the sense of importance, the sense of well-being, that order has for others. Ministry cannot "soar" while leaving our homes in shambles! Ministry cannot be gloriously transparent while we're afraid to raise the shutters at home. Ministry cannot endure the light of scrutiny when we are comfortable in the *darkness* of clutter and chaos at home. We learn from the Word's depiction of creation — if not from leading ladies of house management on the TV — that everything God made and brought into His creation's "household" had a name, a place, and a designated function.

> Everything God made and brought into His creation's "household" had a name, a place, and a designated function.

We often experience clutter in our lives before we experience clutter in our closets. If we cannot say no to invitations and opportunities, we may lack sufficient discernment to eliminate excessive possessions, "baggage," or plain old junk that has accumulated. When we allow tasks, responsibilities, and obligations to pile up and overwhelm us and our families, we neglect family needs and the tasks of continuously building and nurturing elements of those relationships. Then things with no name, out of place, and lacking specific function also weigh us down, sink us in frustration, and sap our strength to do ministry.

But I would imagine the Lord wants us to take power and authority over our households and learn to properly care for those He has placed in our lives. Otherwise, it is equally, if not more, difficult to care for those He has placed within our congregations!

Many women would boldly declare, "But I'm not a good housekeeper!" And possibly, "I just don't have the time for ..." I do not believe, however, that such responsibility has been relinquished or nullified by being called into ministry. We often lack the knowledge that will make things easier or the discipline that can make things better. Perhaps we fret over an inability to coordinate responsibilities with others who reside in the household—spouse, children, renters, housemates, or other relatives.

The quality of the household is everyone's responsibility but the managing of it can be laid at the feet of only one person. Most often, though not always, that is the senior woman in the household, who also might be a *certain woman* called by God, serving Christ Jesus while needing to properly provide for those entrusted to her care and to live peacefully.

I discovered that the Hebrew word *shalom*—and particularly, its equivalent Greek word *eirene*—doesn't simply mean "peace", but rather expresses a greater, richer meaning of the ability to *live life at its best* (according to Marilyn Hickey's *The Names of God*), free from the hurts and hindrances that can often play havoc with such a desire or intent. Life cannot be lived at its best if the very core of our existence is in chaos. House and home need to be not only stabilized but also *organized* to the best degree possible, thus freeing us from wasted time and energy-draining mismanagement. Often I hear the sad saga that begins, "I don't have the time . . ." The truth of the matter is that we all have all of the time we need to live! It's how we choose to use that time that matters most.

Luke's *certain women* project the ability to manage a household—before and more so subsequent to Jesus's invitation to follow Him in ministry. Luke paints a verbal silhouette, identifying these women with absoluteness but with little personal specificity, and then tells us there were "many others." They included Joanna, whose husband was manager of Herod's household, though she was manager of her own. Susanna, whose husband was not named probably due to a lack of prominence or because she was a single woman, also managed a household.

> Many women and men who enter ministry do so without intending to forsake home and household. Yet . . . many do so.

Responsibilities of the call do not negate obligations to family and proper care of loved ones. Many women and men who enter ministry do so without intending to forsake home and household. Yet statistics reflect far too many do so, contributing to divorce and family dysfunction records in the body of Christ to rival those of the world. Often pastoral clergy and staff ministers expect home and family to understand and in that understanding to learn to take care of themselves in the absence—and lack of care—of the ministering spouse or parent. Many in ministry have not learned how to strike that balance or how to involve family in the dimensions of ministry that would prove beneficial for all.

This is where Luke's designation of *certain women* who have been called by Jesus Christ is core to our understanding of the issue. To grab a page from Peter's bio, recall that Jesus told him that if Peter, being a fisherman, would follow Him then Jesus would make him a fisher of men (Mark 1:17). Jesus radically changed Peter. He dramatically changed his life, though he did not reroute Peter's basic abilities as a fisherman. Jesus gave him a new "pond" in which to fish! The phrase *certain women* helps us to further comprehend who we are as women of faith and, hopefully, to grasp with strength our roles and tasks in the kingdom.

Many biblical scholars and theologians want to maintain that Jesus had the women along with them primarily to tend to the details of His comfort and the comfort of the 12 male disciples. They assert that Jewish culture somehow dictated that reality. Yet

Elisabeth Moltman-Wendel, in examination of two other women, references, "Martha had reasons to believe that Mary sat at the feet of Jesus more out of pleasure than for her spiritual advancement. . . [that Martha was afraid that Mary] might continue in this delight and not advance in any way." That is why Martha asked, "Tell her to help me!" Jesus's response in this context points to His interest in women's discipleship: "Mary has chosen what is better and it will not be taken away from her" (Luke 10:42). Jesus settled the dispute, and His words provide fresh insight not only on how He viewed the women He called and the issue of managing our households well but also with respect to three important dimensions of His ministry: discipleship, hospitality, and time.

Discipleship. Luke 8:1–3 clearly demonstrates that Jesus held women at a similar level as even the Twelve or other disciples, meaning that when He was in their presence, His presence was the essential thing—nothing else was as important for the benefit of the person. He lovingly rebuked Martha and affirmed Mary's choice to sit at His feet and learn from Him. While He was in their presence, the first order of the day was "to learn of Him" (Matthew 11:29). For He was shaping even these two women into beloved disciples. He was reconfiguring their primary orientation from hospitality and attention to the mundane and human cares to a grander orientation towards God's kingdom. Jesus was to be not just a part of their lives but the very focus of their lives.

Hospitality. Hospitality is the hallmark of Judaism with much Scripture imploring and instructing Israelites in the proper care of even the stranger at their doors. All Jews lived with that set of expectations about caring for beloved guests or strangers in their midst. For God, there was virtually no difference. As early as Genesis, God began to *sow the seeds* of hospitality to strangers by requiring His chosen people to *remember* they, too, were once *strangers* in a foreign land and would be also even in the land He planned to give them! Our Christian hospitality, perhaps, lacks that dimension of sensitivity that we, too, are *sojourners* — strangers to and in this land. That understanding should hopefully inspire us in the richer, meaningful ways of providing hospitality to other strangers who enter our doors.

Needless to say, there were cultural traditions as well that Martha was dutifully attempting to fulfill. She had the physical and practical well-being of her houseguests uppermost in her mind and nothing was going to diminish her degree of proficiency in skill or will to make their comfort and care her priority. Martha is not to be faulted. Martha — and the Marthas of today — can enlarge and sensitize us to the greater needs of guests in our homes.

According to Moltmann-Wendel, Rudolf Bultman posits Mary against Martha by declaring, "In Mary, then, we find a portrayal of the first stage of faith, beyond which her sister had advanced ... Mary does not have Martha's certainty." According to John 11:21 and 11:32, both Martha and Mary were equal in the faith that they expressed in the Lord at the graveside of their brother Lazarus. Their greater difference was in how they chose to live out that faith and have their faith nurtured and sustained at Jesus's feet.

Many have realized already that there is a duality of both Mary and Martha in us as women. Though we might develop one side or the other poorly, it is still there as a vital (though perhaps dormant) part of who we are. My sister accompanied me to many of my speaking engagements over the years. Whenever they would acknowledge her presence in the congregation, often the person would compare us to Mary and Martha, always to her chagrin. I knew we would talk about it on the drive home after service. It eventually became a joke between us, though tinged with a bit of pain and seriousness. My sister said, "I'm *tired* of being Martha!"

It's not that she had to be *Martha*. It's that she chose to be. It wasn't that she couldn't be Mary. It was that, even as a believer, she chose not to prioritize her life around the Lord Jesus Christ. For her, cleaning came before church, dish washing came before devotions, bed making came before Bible reading, getting dressed was more important than doing devotions, and making money limited her time in and for meditation. As a nurse, she could easily work double shifts and more, but too often found it difficult to clear even 15 minutes to be alone with the Lord. When the hospital called, she would move heaven and earth to get there speedily. Washing clothes was more important than witnessing. She lived a nominal Christian life because she chose to do so.

In my life, I chose "*what is better*" as my focus, holding on to the words that Jesus declared, "It will not be taken from her." In doing so over the years — much to my delight — I discovered how much *Martha* was an integral dimension of *Mary*. My sister and I did ultimately agree, and it became "us against them" when they would call her *Martha*. Often I would follow up with the comment, "But there is so much of *Mary* in this *Martha*." I believe that's the composite of every *certain woman*.

Having been in numerous private homes in 43 of our 50 states and in 42 different countries, some as many as 15 to 20 times, I realize hospitality standards vary greatly. Sometimes in the poorest of homes, hospitality is more lavish in its attentiveness to needs and the freedom bestowed on the guests within the household. Whereas in some well-established, well-appointed homes, the warmth in hospitality is not as automatic. Though hosts and hostesses make guests physically comfortable amidst the evident opulence, significant warmth towards the guests may be missing.

While I was growing up, my parents welcomed many a stranger into our home. The most enduring memory of strangers visiting our home is of two men from India. They were brought to our home by my mother's brother-in-law, a merchant seaman at the time. These two men were on shore leave with him. At age seven, I'm not certain I had ever heard of their country. They were strangers, indeed, to our household. From a child's perspective, they talked funny and dressed in funny clothes. I can still remember my giggles and my sister's. But the lesson my mother taught in our very modest home was to always "treat guests as family and family as guests!"

In all of the hospitality that I have longed for (in its absence) or enjoyed the most (in its presence) throughout these many years of travel, no other rule seems to have worked better. For the first part of my mother's wisdom — "treat guest as family" — bestows immediate trust and honors the personhood of the guest while the second — "treat family as guests" — assumes some good level of trust is already established and moves toward the opportunity to lavish love and provide finer care of needs.

Time. Christ came to spend time with people so they could learn to properly invest their time into the lives of others for the glory of God. Relationships require time together. That's what

Martha was missing and Mary grasped right away. What was most important? Not the chair He sat in or the condition of the room or the lavishness of the meal He would receive. *He* was important! His presence was their benefit and His words (conversation) were the treasure of the moment—not the fried chicken or the hot rolls!

The Guest and what He had to give was the supreme treasure that defined the visitation. For any visitation, it's how you spend your time together during the visit that will leave the most indelible impression on the hearts and in the memories of guests. Jesus gave to Mary and Martha the lesson in presence that He had come to give to all disciples. What a lesson! What power! What a new reality! What care! What love! Mary had chosen the good part and it would "not be taken away from her."

Theological and biblical scholars make a second mistake in asserting that Jesus's teachings to these two women are isolated and seemingly have little to any merit of learning for all disciples. To do that is to successfully diminish the great lessons of this text. To underscore the principles involved a bit more, we might want to place two brothers in a similar scene at a carpenter's workshop instead of inside of the house. If one brother had stopped his work and sat at the feet of Jesus while the other continued to craft furniture, what do you expect the reaction of Jesus might have been? The message of this text has an impact on every believer as well as the work of the kingdom of God.

experiencing new ways of being

What was one of the new ways of being that became the hallmark of Christianity? In Acts, Luke declared that "believers had everything in common" (Acts 2:44). In other words, they had learned how to share and provide for one another far beyond their cultural boundaries or religious inclinations. Beyond the social and economic requirements that might have impinged upon biblical mandates.

The Luke 8:1–3 text spreads across the width and breadth of Jesus Christ's ministry, providing a colorful ribbonlike "thread" of insight into His ministry. It shows that His ministry is never as limited as some have claimed, and with this text, it begins for some and continues for others to manifest a collectiveness of callings across the width and breadth of Christendom.

For His entrance into Jerusalem to celebrate Passover, Jesus sent some of the Twelve ahead to prepare, and part of that preparation was for the Passover meal. He did not send the women to prepare the table or the food or the room where they would fellowship together. Rather, He chose two of the Twelve. Joel Green comments in The New International Commentary on the New Testament: *The Gospel of Luke*, "to serve usually has the connotation of 'waiting tables' in Luke-Acts, though this practice comes to serve as a metaphor for leadership." Perhaps, then, we can connect appropriate preparation with an appropriate quality of hospitality, which becomes suggestive of a quality of leadership offered to the body of Christ! Such is the quality of *certain women who manage their households well.*

It's not about being wealthy, but it's about appropriately handling the wealth we already have. Perhaps there is no greater place where the gospel is needed to be preached, taught, and modeled than in our homes today, to clearly exemplify the transformative power of the risen Christ. He is able to bring order out of chaos and to enable us to treat our family members as guests in the sense of our quality of care for them. He enables us to continue to carve out the time to sit at His feet in meditative repose, in order to more fully absorb who He wants to be in us today.

eflections

Household management is not much unlike the management of the universe. God *spoke* to chaos and brought order to it! The will (choice) and knowledge of maintaining order are paramount in managing a household or the universe. The first is under your authority, the second is under God's authority. Reflect upon these two realities and decide where you are in the ordering of your life, your family, and your household.

It's not a matter of having time but what you choose to do with the time that you do have. More importantly, how can you free yourself of stuff that drains your energy, which works to diminish your time that could be put into better management of your household? What do you need to let go?

What quality of hospitality do you offer those who come into your home?

*P*rayer

certain women
*lose their fear
of difference*

Culture — FAR MORE THAN RELIGION — CAN BOTH GREATLY HIGHLIGHT and intensify our human differences. Religion more decidedly has a coalescing, if not unifying, effect while culture often leads us into the stratification of people within the same culture and fosters a sense of exclusivity relative to those of cultures other than our own. Religion can certainly foster the same ways of being in the world, but the pharisaical approach is totally rejected by Jesus Christ. "Culture" would always be in opposition to the spoken desire of Jesus Christ: that we (as believers) be *one*. In preparation for entertaining such a request, losing our fear of difference is fundamental.

Tyrants thrive and survive by perverting difference and exclusivity. Politicians fail or succeed by distinguishing themselves from other politicians to win favor from the populace, for good or ill. Teachers' pets gain the largesse of their teacher through deference to the teacher and an occasional proverbial apple or two. Now none of that is totally bad, but all of it sorely fails to accentuate the reality that God made us all far more alike than different. The contextual trappings of human beings certainly can vary drastically. However, on nearly every internal scale, scientists have confirmed many times that we are far more alike than different. Such commonalities, beyond the physical, should serve as relief from fear of difference based on one's language, dress, or geographical location.

All of the differences we detect within the church today were potentialities within the disciples of Jesus when He walked upon the earth. Personality differences, religious differences, ethnic differences, social differences, and more! Yet we still proclaim, "Greater is he that is in us, than he that is in the world!" (1 John 4:4 KJV). The power of that biblical proclamation loses its resonance when we give in to all of the elements that "the world" proclaims should divide us as human beings. These *certain women* and the Twelve did not have the reality of that written verse, 1 John 4:4, but it is evident that one of the Twelve, John, had the truth of it impressed upon his spirit. John had walked the road of ministry with Jesus, encountering many different challenges, obstacles, hindrances, and difficulties along the way.

If that was a reality for John, it had not come as an afterthought beyond the Resurrection; he had seen the evidence of that reality while on the journey with Jesus! These *certain women* as well would have gleaned such a great truth as they encountered people and circumstances within one of the most diversely populated regions at that time: Galilee. Judaism alone was "splintered" into at least six groups: Sadducees, Pharisees, Essenes, Zealots, disciples of John the Baptist, and the followers of Jesus! We tend to think of all the disciples as one monolithic group of Jews, not grasping the variety of beliefs, practices, and religious behaviors that divided them, let alone the many differences within other spheres of their lives.

Of Mary Magdalene, Joanna, and Susanna, it seems that probably only Mary Magdalene was a Jewess; a reality that would have thrown significant cultural and religious differences into the mix of their relationships. Such differences did not portend danger, only difficulties that would have rendered certain aspects of these relationships a little more challenging, but not devastating.

With full intention, God built a quality and quantity of differences into creation. Even seven different days, innumerably different animals and types of flowers and foliage, and two human beings—male and female—embody myriad differences. God loves difference! Is it not time that we learn to love what God loves? He looked at all of those differences imbedded within His creation and pronounced them, Good! So why do we see them as bad? Why do we need to diminish people because of their differences and even feel diminished because of our own differences? How glorious are those differences!

These *certain women* would have first intuited their own differences as they entered the group and began to travel that road of ministry with Jesus. They would have also noticed differences among the other women as well as among the Twelve. But there was someone among them all who made *the* difference, Jesus. He was the bridge they could traverse in and out of one another's life regardless of all the differences. This predates Paul's declaration, "So we, being many, are one body in Christ, and every one members one of another" (Romans 12:5 KJV).

But perhaps the supreme biblical declaration about our differences is in Galatians:

> *For ye are all the children of God by faith in Christ Jesus. For as many of you as have been baptized into Christ have put on Christ. There is neither Jew nor*

Greek, there is neither bond nor free, there is neither male nor female for ye are all one in Christ Jesus.
—GALATIONS 3:26–28 (KJV)

This passage is not declaring that these major human differences do not exist. Quite the contrary! Even mentioning them heightens our awareness of their existence. However, Paul was questing for and developing awareness about the greater reality that these differences recede into the commonality we have in Christ! No other power that I have ever encountered delivers in its call for, promise about, or pronouncements of the greater goal of oneness and the recognition of our human commonalities.

Such sentiments didn't begin after Pentecost, but were an inherent part of the more than three-year ministry of Christ Jesus. Then He went to the Cross to seal the salvation that made it possible for us to move beyond our differences through our faith in Him. The Galatians passage clearly shows that *faith* trumps *fear* every time! So in our faith, we should be capable of transforming and becoming free of every fear—including the fear of difference. Estrangement is in total opposition to the purpose of Christ on the earth! God wants us to learn how to embrace one another regardless of our inherent or contextual differences.

distinguished by a different love

I do not believe Jesus would have allowed the disciples and the *certain women* with them to ostracize one another for any reason at all. He was on earth *to free us* from such alienating thoughts and behaviors. He was on earth to bring about *a new creation.*

It is appropriate to be distinguished one from another for practical reasons, spiritual anointing, or religious roles. However, it is a very different matter to separate ourselves as believers based upon racial constructs, ethnicity, economics, education, culture, and other factors.

But how do we believers progress beyond such behavior? First we must condemn it within ourselves and help to address it within other believers. We need to grow out of our own small spheres and narrowly prescribed corners of the world within which we purport to like and accept only that which looks like, thinks like, and behaves like us. We can move out into the broader spaces of the kingdom that spans the globe to include everyone who has named the name of Jesus Christ as Savior and Lord!

Paul was questing for and developing awareness about the greater reality that these differences recede into the commonality we have in Christ!

Black/White. Nearly 10 years ago, I colored my hair blonde. Some folk literally questioned whether I, an African American woman, was "trying to be white" as though God had exclusively given to European Americans that hair color. For me it was, indeed, spiritual, in that for a couple of years prior to the decision, I sensed, *You need to put light around your face.* Initially I wondered what it meant. I couldn't conveniently wear a light bulb on my head nor could I wear a light-colored hat on my head 24/7. What did this instruction mean?

When it finally hit me to lighten my hair, I was initially afraid. Once I did it, the change ushered me into a new level of freedom in the Lord because of the obedience. God will test us in some small, even obscure things before He leads us into some bigger matters that will test what He has put in us! For many of us, it's far easier to grasp the need for change of the larger stages of our lives—morals, work ethics, race, economics, and so on. However, some of our greatest spiritual lessons do not always emanate from the greater spheres of our lives. Jesus used seeds to teach many all-encompassing lessons about life well lived. He pointed to the birds to teach us to trust in God for our well-being.

European Americans have for eons enjoyed sunbathing while being laughed at, sneered at, and even derided by nonwhites relative to their "trying to be black" during the summer while "hating people with darkened skin during the spring, fall, and winter." Well, God did not give to people of African, Asian, or other descent exclusive claim on beautifully browned skin color either!

Differences. Get over them. Get beyond them. Get around them. They create a prison within themselves, and Jesus Christ came to free us from such bondage! "If the Son sets you free, you will be free indeed" (John 8:36). "The truth will set you free" (John 8:32). To enlarge our capacity to love, we must begin to become free of the encumbrance of the fears of difference among human beings.

Personality. Perhaps personality differences were the strongest beyond the religious differences inherent within those who followed Jesus. Oh, what a challenge then and now for us as human beings to get beyond such differences and learn to work together far more effectively.

A previous colleague of mine was quite high-strung, to the degree that I sometimes dreaded being around her. In those moments, even "night and day" could not have defined the contrast in our personalities! Oh, how I prayed. I really liked her and wanted to get along but found that *difference* nearly intolerable. One day in prayer, I was led to reflect upon her good qualities and excellent work. Then the Spirit of the Lord encouraged me to "follow that line that connected her work with her personality." I admitted then and now that perhaps I had known few other more detail-oriented, energetic, capable people. Many had possessed various aspects of the three qualities, but few had had those three qualities to the same degree and in as great balance as did Cricket White.

Continuing to reflect prayerfully, God helped me to "see" her more holistically in contrast to the compartmentalizing of her personality quirks I had successfully achieved just to get along. I'm a thinker. She's a doer. We both had the opposite's capacities—just not to the same degree. We began to talk it out and quickly understood one another on a far deeper level, a level that brought acceptance and collegiality in a more profound way.

She declared to me that she literally shook whenever I would announce in some of our planning meetings, "I've got an idea. What about . . . ?" because it often seemed to her to be on the scale of attempting "to put a tent over the Swiss Alps," and she knew she would be the one who had to find all the pegs! In the moment of sharing the idea, *pegs* would not have entered my mind. They would have later but not within seconds of intuiting the idea. Oh, how differently we were wired together within our personalities and their practical manifestations! But God had made it so, and we agreed that we two needed each other. Recognizing that she wasn't the idea person (thinking way outside of the box), neither was I the "peg" person (intuiting every minute detail within nanoseconds of hearing the idea), we knew we were part of God's larger plan to accomplish greater things together, differences aside.

I have carried that lesson into each relationship since then, and it has allowed me to enjoy being able to explore the richer side of difference ever since. Such a process is part and parcel of losing one's *fear* of difference. Where do we begin? I have heard it said that what we hate in others is what we often reject or abhor within ourselves. What I have witnessed is nearly just the opposite: what we long for within ourselves is what we tend to negate (dislike/reject) others for having already. The poor hate the rich, the uneducated hate the educated, the fat folk hate the skinny, and on and on! If we could only establish some quality of relationship with the one who possesses that which is different, we might gain a wonderful benefit that would enhance our lives.

In Christ, the statement "there is neither bond nor free" (Galatians 3:28 KJV) is a call to move beyond our fears or rejection of difference, to know that His all-consuming power is plenty sufficient to create this new level of spiritual maturity. God has made us different for good reasons, not bad. We miss His intended blessings when we negate differences that might not sit too well with us initially. When we probe within ourselves for the reasons why, then we can allow the Spirit of the Lord to show us the connections between personality and proclivities.

reconciled to differences

How many differences might there be among the entire human race? There are probably far more than we could ever know or enumerate. The differences we know fairly well may not be fresh in our minds until we encounter someone in whom those differences are prominent and impress or distress us. It is at times even difficult to handle the idiosyncrasies or differences we can identify within ourselves, much less those in other people. But try as we may, it is difficult to understand such fears that become the basis for "isms" of all kinds: racism, sexism, ageism, and more.

Many studies have shown that human beings are far more similar than dissimilar from one another.

Many studies have shown that human beings are far more similar than dissimilar from one another. Yet politics, culture, and religion have each worked far more diligently to separate human beings based on difference than to help us bond around our similarities. That has not changed over the millennia of civilization and, if anything, has more greatly intensified.

For far more than 20 years, I have worked professionally in the area of racial reconciliation. It often has been difficult to comprehend why folk were more comfortable separating within and over certain racial, political, social, or religious differences. I've often wondered, *Why are the lessons that helped us learn to embrace people—beyond the differences they manifested—so difficult?* Then I realized that the lessons were not difficult to rationally comprehend, but the spiritual power that made us able to embrace and apply what we had learned was a far different matter.

In our contemporary church life, we often are more prone to declaring who we are—from pedigree to profession—rather than exemplifying interest in and openness to who others gathered around us are. These *certain women* who were called by Jesus made history not only in their response to Him and service to the kingdom but also in their social encounters with both genders among His disciples. It probably was no easy task, but Luke does not provide for us any insight into the difficulties they may have encountered.

Yet today we probably struggle with the same issues they may have struggled with as they brought their faith to bear upon the work they were called to do: issues of authority and power, experience and expertise, cultural preferences and ethnic traditions, and more. But how do we move beyond that morass? How do we free ourselves and move beyond that forest in which we have been lost for so long? I would offer that God did not *give* us such differences to become the basis for division within the church; quite the contrary, our differences should become the foundation upon which a stronger sense of commonality in the church is established!

Those Jesus called together were as diverse as a small cadre of women could be, making it all the more incumbent on them to not only recognize their differences but to move from such recognition towards a sense of commonality and common commitment to the Master's plans as they traveled from city to city. Socially diverse, perhaps spiritually diverse, and most likely ethnically diverse, there would have been much to get over and get beyond in their everyday encounters with one another. Not unlike us, they had to learn about and from each other while learning about and from the Lord.

Certain women seem to have a higher level of expectation for their own lives and for the service they render in response to the Christ, who has given them legitimacy of service in the church and beyond.

In our churches today, we most often totally neglect the reality of how radical Jesus was in His day! Jewish women were not patsies—they knew when to be quiet and unassuming, but they knew when to get their point across as well. Whatever their customs, Jesus was breaking through the boundaries and parameters of those customs just by having called them to minister with Him in the region of Galilee. They spoke. They shared. They witnessed. They served. They bonded with Him and with one another, laying the very foundation of what was yet to come in Jerusalem: "All the believers were together and had everything in common" (Acts 2:44). Mentally, we have relegated that "everything in common" to *after* Pentecost, neglecting to follow the antecedents to the faithful having been able to do just that—to release personal belongings into the realm of sufficiency for all. It is not impossible for me to believe that the very seeds of that were planted as, collectively, they ministered from Jerusalem to Galilee and back!

What challenges the Lord faced in endeavoring to bring some level of harmony in the relationships of the Twelve as well as among and with those *certain women* whom He invited to join His band of itinerant proclaimers! From town to town, from house to house, and field to field and in spaces and places large enough for the crowds that gathered, Jesus had to have been concerned not only about their witness but also about the quality of their relationships. Jesus drew strong, capable people into His ministry—not just the physically stalwart but those who had levels of spiritual maturity as well. They may have been new to Him, but their faith in God was not necessarily new, giving Jesus much to build upon.

The stronger the personality, the greater the possibilities of conflict and the presence of heightened differences. Folks, as

There was no aggressive competing to sit at Jesus's right hand.

much in ministry and the church as in the world, seem timid and afraid of dealing with conflict and differences within the ranks of the leadership.

As *certain women,* it should not be named among us that we find it easier *not* to get along than to get along. Too often we seem defined by conflicting agendas than by the camaraderie that characterized the women who walked with Jesus. Their only agenda was to support His ministry in all the practical ways and allow their lives to radiate His power to onlookers and learners, bringing glory to God! We know that the complete story of these *certain women* is not told in these three verses that are the basic text for this book. However, I would believe that, had there been great problems among the female constituents of those who traveled with Jesus, Luke would have conveyed as much. From his vantage point, they shared in the ministry of Jesus from beginning to end.

There is no mention of discord of any type among them. There was no aggressive competing to sit at Jesus's right hand or any attempts to manage or gain authority over one another's life as Peter tried with John. Perhaps they had found that everyone who comes to Jesus has been delivered of something and freed from being a captive of sin. Since that is the case, perhaps these *certain women* saw no reason to "look down the nose" at the other women. Neither had they the need to "raise the elite eyebrow" as they looked at one another.

Having encountered *certain women* on four continents and in 42 countries, my fear of difference is gone! I have no sense of being less than or more than because the ground at the foot of the cross is level. Every believer is looking up at the Lord and not down at each other. All humanity stands before the cross, not a millimeter higher or lower than another. Such a realization is so freeing because I am—and they are—in Christ Jesus our Lord! Oh how different we are from one another in skills, abilities, life experiences, political perspectives, individual needs, and more, but such differences never qualify us to be valued as more than or less than anyone else within the kingdom of God.

Some years ago, I began a rose garden. Although each type had its own beautiful color, texture, petal shape, and stem length, they all had to be planted in soil, watered, pruned, and fertilized regularly, and all required the sun to bloom. Having given them all the same care, how I reveled in seeing the differences they produced thereafter. Can you imagine the joy of the Lord with all that He has poured into our salvation that we, too, should bask in His glory and bloom in the beautiful abilities He has blessed us to have? No room for envy, just the impetus to become who He fully intended each of us to be.

You are the only one who can first know that you are *there*—that you have discovered what is true for you and true within you as you live out your faith in Jesus Christ. When each of us reaches that point, we lose any need to compete with anyone else socially, culturally, economically, religiously, or spiritually. We gain the greater capacity to approach, affirm, and applaud folks who exhibit greater abilities. We begin to do what is real for self, and in such moments, we enjoy the strength of being who God created us to be. This thinking becomes a gateway for God to bring new blessings into our lives and what I call "a holy exit" for other things that we or the Lord might not be as pleased about in our lives. New confidence emerges. New ways of thinking and behaving happen automatically because we are no longer making decisions about how we compare or stack up with other people! We give what we know we have and welcome any other to do the same.

Such realizations also allow us to partner with God in some brand-new ways. God has been waiting for us to realize that we are not someone else but that we are the beautiful, wonder-filled creation on which He placed His stamp of approval: *It is good!* Because of that discovery straight out of Genesis, we are no longer comfortable with what we may have been trying to become, but we have reached such a joyous threshold of authenticity that who we really are blossoms and unfolds in myriad and miraculous ways. It is, then, that authenticity that God begins to use to draw people to us rather than us pursuing folk who may or may not want us within their sphere.

Certain women take such realities and shape very different relationships as they work together for the cause of Christ. We begin to value more honestly and deeply what each one brings into those relationships and, hopefully, begin to eliminate those comparative barriers that prevent us from hearing either the mind or heart of those who are so different from us—those whom we previously thought to be better. We find that we can work with anybody. It is not that everyone else has changed to allow such a possibility; but rather, we have changed and have no further need to either diminish or to revere others on the basis of superfluous details about their life or inflated ideas about our own.

There is no magic age that one can reach for this process to be initiated. It can happen at any age or stage because its beginning is prompted by one's faith, not by one's accomplishments or ultimate possessions. Actively questing for and joyously pursuing all that God wants us to be leaves no time to continuously review someone else's life to see how we compare with him or her. What freedom! What deliverance! What liberation! All brought by Jesus, who continues to bring this and more into the lives of *certain women*.

eflections

What are your greatest fears in or about other people that make you feel uncomfortable or afraid?

Can you trace these feelings/thoughts/ideas back to their original source to connect with the experience or other person(s) who initiated such fears in you?

What additional information can you find to help put these fears to rest, which would aid you in accepting the biblical mandate and declaration that we be one? (See John 17:21)

*P*rayer

certain women
know how
to become one

THESE *CERTAIN WOMEN* WERE A FORCE WITHIN A FORCE! THEY WERE at the Master's feet, developing and being *retooled* for effective ministry, as were the Twelve. As Jesus pulled them together, they must have realized they could not be obedient *to* and cooperative *with* Him *and* follow personal agendas. They must have learned the essence of following Jesus: "Let this mind be in you" (Philippians 2:5 KJV). What a force they created! What a foundation they established! What cataclysmic changes they manifested, because they had a singular purpose: to become *one* in the work of the Master. *One* power, *one* purpose, and *one* plan. You and I are the results of their effective work over 2,000 years ago!

With the exception of Judas's, God allowed no other plan to render their individual efforts unsuccessful. Together they sowed the seeds of faith and evidently were able to put aside their differences to do the work of Christ. They didn't hear just His words; they "heard" the greatest quest of His heart for them: that they be *one*. They could not just mouth what He taught them; they became the models of His truth and power.

Luke researched them from the time of the earlier days of Jesus's ministry to the earliest days of the church. Luke's words take on greater meaning for us in view of the fact that he wrote two biblical books chronicling not only the gospel but the birth of the church and the quality of relationships that characterized those embryonic moments. Luke–Acts is "the longest contribution by a single writer to the New Testament. It presents the story of what Jesus did and taught first in His earthly life (the gospel) and then as the exalted Christ and Lord through His followers (Acts)," according to Richard Longenecker in *Into God's Presence*.

That provides Luke with not just a literary vantage point, but with a perspective not found in the works of other Gospel writers, such as Luke's three verses about the *certain women*. Their names—except for Mary Magdalene—are not mentioned by the other Gospel writers, though some believe that Luke might have used those writers as sources for parts of his Gospel.

Although the following words may have been penned by Paul—"So we, being many, are one body in Christ, and every one members one of another" (Romans 12:5 KJV*)*—the sentiments are expressed in the writings of Luke–Acts. Within this block of material, these women's names may not be profusely mentioned, but there is no doubt that the impact of their presence—having been personally trained by the Master and having walked with Him, served him, and supported the efforts of His ministry—made them some of the unsung heroines of the infant church. *Certain women* helped insure the sense of family and oneness that characterized new believers as Luke describes in Acts. Within those experiences with the Master, I believe that a sense of oneness was born within their spirits that transcended their differences as women and as followers of Jesus. Therefore, it is important for *certain women* today to affirm the oneness—the commonality—in themselves, of which Jesus is the source.

And so, these women found a new sense of solidarity in one another relationally as they had found in Jesus spiritually. Because of the profound changes in their lives wrought by the Savior, their relationships with one another within the parameters of that salvation could not have been simple or simplistic. It's not a solidarity *against* anyone, but *for* and with the Lord!

All of us didn't grow up the same way nor did we encounter Jesus at identical junctions of our journeys. But after we met Jesus for ourselves, all of us were the same: heaven bound! But Satan keeps our focus too earthbound, too ego driven — hats, white dresses, who's president, who's not president, who lives where and drives what — stuff of little to no significance or consequence in balance with the work Jesus calls us into and gives us responsibility to do as His kingdom servants. *Certain women* endeavor to move beyond the externals, the artificial religious trappings, as they move toward the simple things that make us *one* and toward the more profound realities that can solidify that oneness.

What I believe serves to hinder this oneness is that too many women have thought of biblical women as only serving the needs of males in the group. That's not biblically correct. Neither is believing that even then women allowed themselves to not have any influence, impact, or effect upon the males in their lives, be it husband, brother, father, or son! On the Web site www.crosswalk.com, I came across this quote recently that should help to highlight this matter for us: "We should note how Jesus began to remove the fetters of custom which bound women, and to bring about a condition of . . . freedom."

Jesus yearned for oneness to characterize His followers. In His high priestly prayer in John 17, Jesus makes it so clear that there is nothing greater He wants to characterize His followers than that *oneness* He says will be a shining beacon to the world, signaling that He has already come, bringing salvation to all!

Yet it's that *oneness* that continues to stymie the followers of Jesus. We seem to enjoy singling out our differences, heightening our individuality even in the midst of team efforts. Our service to the church, and the kingdom, takes a divisive "hit." Jesus wanted the essence of what He had with the Father to be the exemplar for relationships among believers—a *oneness* that served to spiritually *season* those earthbound relationships. He knew that such a quality would demonstrate to the world the power of the living Christ in our lives.

In heaven, Jesus would be our central focus, and we would do well to insure that He is our central focus here on the earth as we engage in bringing His kingdom to the world! *There* we will no longer inflict any more pain on one another for there will be no more tears; yet *here* in the church, there seems to be far too much pain as political games abound and finding ways to marginalize or exclude one another from church leadership and functioning seems the order of the day.

A deacon once was proudly sharing his recent encounter with a disheveled man just outside of our church building. He declared that he invited him to worship the next Sunday and the man declined the invitation because of a lack of a suit to wear. The deacon immediately offered him a suit or two of his own, seeing that they were nearly the same size. The man still rejected the invitation. The deacon walked on into his church meeting, disappointed, having negative thoughts about the man who had just rejected his kind invitation to come and worship with them. It was difficult to help him to understand that the man wasn't rejecting the invitation, nor was he rejecting the suits. The man was rejecting the deacon's rejection of him. Why couldn't he have come as he was? Why couldn't he be accepted at the level of "decency" he could afford?

The deacon was afraid of that "difference" coming into *his* church! His cultural orientation to "judge a book by its cover" (the man by the clothes he wears) led him to reject the person for whom Christ died and, in essence, *close the door of the church* to him. He successfully removed from that man any level of acceptance. I still pray for that man now: that God would send someone — anyone — to lavish on his life true acceptance in the church of Jesus Christ. For in that one encounter, the deacon, the believer, rejected all of the potentialities God had put into that man and that he could contribute to that church. Our fear of *difference* often leads us into counterproductive ways than what the gospel espouses for winning the lost.

What is it in this *oneness* that is so powerful a witness to the world? What is the substance of such oneness that seemingly makes it so difficult to either achieve it or sustain it for long? Where can we find even the will to make this oneness happen? What might fuel such oneness that will enable us to desire it rather than languish in our sense of spiritual independence?

The German word *gestalt* can be quite informative here. It provides the insight that the whole, or totality, of anything is greater than the sum of its parts. It has taken psychological experts decades to arrive at such thinking and then, subsequently, for us all to benefit from that comprehensive thought. Two of my mentors contribute greatly to this thought in their book, which chronicles the summation of their ministries and celebrates their togetherness.

Commenting on the proclivity of couples to compete with one another, Henry Mitchell discloses that he and his beloved companion, Ella Pearson Mitchell, "have a strange habit of identifying with each other's victories more than we enjoy our own." Virtually all of their married lives as they have traveled far to proclaim Christ, church folk have attempted to pit them against one another, compare them more unfavorably against one another, or try to exalt one of them over the other.

They were the ones who have stopped that kind of thinking as people spoke such thoughts, because they were not in the ministry of Jesus Christ to compete with one another in preaching, teaching, or writing but have endeavored to support, encourage, and sustain one another in every way they deemed possible. Together, the two of them became a *gestalt* in that the two together became "more than the sum of (their) parts," as reflected in his comment. In symbolic numbers, it amounts to something such as $1 + 1 = 5$. Their synergy spurred surprising creativity. Their Lord joined and enriched them immeasurably to become far more together than they could ever be separately or competitively.

I would imagine that such oneness characterized the journeys of these *certain women* into and throughout Galilee, in and out of various towns where Jesus took the motley crew. So what hinders that oneness from characterizing our ability to work for the Master? Everything from low tolerance levels to egomania range as possibilities; but other than the obvious ones, what are some other real culprits within female relationships that prevent them from being the quality we long for? Could beauty be one, or the perceived lack thereof? Could physical shape be one or the lack of being statuesque? Could preventing your friends from being friends of another person simply because you don't like that other person or because you have first laid claim on them as your friends be such a culprit? Trust?

Reckon with the reality that no matter where we are, we are surrounded by the presence of those who intentionally or unintentionally (historically, culturally, biblically, and so on) infuse our relationships with a level of competition. Sadly, to a disappointing degree, women's relationships within the church—in spiritually unhealthy ways—are driven and influenced by those who often are more influenced by culture than by the transforming power of the gospel.

> Certain women are challenged to honestly face these and other negative influences on sisterly relationships in the church.

Certain women are challenged to honestly face these and other negative influences on sisterly relationships in the church. We will not nor can we hope to achieve that *oneness* Jesus longed for us and all believers to have until this is understood. The negative influence of women upon sisterly relationships is part of the same continuum.

What are the spiritual components of that *oneness* that Jesus envisioned? That His followers would first understand how they reflected *His* mission (Luke 4:18) and not their personal agendas:

• Preach the good news
• Proclaim freedom
• Recover sight
• Release the oppressed
• Proclaim the Lord's favor

These are the tasks but, before undertaking these five tasks, He declared, "The Spirit of the Lord is on me," which would be the generating power giving Him the ability to do these five tasks. Additionally, God had anointed Jesus to do what He was sent to do just as the Lord anoints us to do what we are sent to do! That anointing is not only our generating power but also the power to bind us together in the *oneness* that clarifies and characterizes the tasks.

Preach the good news. We've become so acclimated to style over substance, voice tone over content, that we've considered preaching competitive rather than complementary with everyone preaching good news! Yes, God uses personality in proclamation, but far more important than the vast dimensions and manifestations of one's personality is the presence of God's anointing!

Jesus was never in a pulpit so we cannot limit His pronouncements to pulpit preaching even in our contemporary times. Jesus's preaching was to small groups, with few exceptions, and into relationships He developed with people from His initial declaration in the Temple until His return to the Father. We tend to consider the Luke 4:18 text with too pastoral a tint on it. Broadening our idea of where we as believers *preach,* we must realize that far more *preaching* is done beyond the pulpit than from the pulpit. Therefore, it is incumbent on us to discern the qualities Jesus poured into individual relationships with His disciples rather than continuing to see His proclamation as tantamount to a pulpit-only declaration.

Far too often, we damage relationships in the church because we preach judgment instead of good news, being quicker to condemn another believer rather than commend!

Proclaim freedom. How can we be so bound ourselves and be able to proclaim *freedom* to others? The need to control others in the faith emanates from a spirit of religious bondage. We must first be free in our spirits to share the gospel's message of freedom to others!

Recover sight. This is not sight we have lost but the inability *to see* because we are focused on the wrong things!

Release the oppressed. Too often we bind people afresh with our harshness, keeping them in bondage through negative attitudes we portray, seeking to control *them* rather than disciplining ourselves through the power of the gospel! If we could taste the freedom that Jesus brings to us through our faith, we then could enjoy setting others at liberty to be and become all that God intends, *setting at liberty* all of their gifts, talents, and abilities for the cause of the kingdom.

Proclaim the Lord's favor. Jesus verbally chastised Peter when Peter sought to "manage" John's behavior instead of partnering with him as we ultimately see him doing over in Acts. Peter could not pronounce the Lord's favor upon John's life as Jesus had spoken into Peter's life. In that moment, Jesus quite strongly asked Peter, "If I will that he tarry till I come, what is that to [you]?" (John 21:22 KJV). Jesus takes responsibility for His relationship with each believer!

Our relationships within the church should be far better, far more meaningful, than those outside of that fellowship even given that some are at varying stages of spiritual development. We tend to negate them by *painting* them with a large swathe of pseudo religion rather than genuine Christianity: *I'm blessed! We're blessed!* When a more categorical response might be more appropriate. *Certain women* are genuine women with no need of pretense and no pretense of need. Truth is our banner. The Word is our shield! His presence in our lives *is* our power. And the anointing of His Spirit is the gift that makes us one!

John 17 is poignant and powerful in its message of oneness—as capable today to refocus the church as it was when Jesus spoke those words giving the disciples the perspective through which to shape the church. The pathos I sense in the words of our Lord is at times somewhat overwhelming, particularly when coupled with more than 50 years of conscious involvement within Christendom and the church. The ways He defined and lifted up His desire for our oneness within this chapter, or "high priestly prayer," as it is often referred to, amazes my mind and spirit.

I've particularly seen women who were not academically trained struggle to be "the same as" or "as good as" women who were. They don't realize that they constantly affirm their *inferiority* in the process because they could never *be the same* without benefit of similar educational experiences and accomplishments! Knowledge and the experience of education do, indeed, make one different. Where we fall into the cultural trap is in believing that it makes us "better." It is what God puts into us and our lives that makes us better, not how we can mimic others. Thus we throw ourselves into the sociocultural/religious-spiritual battle of self-definition because,

Certain women are genuine women with no need of pretense and no pretense of need.

within the church, we are constantly pitted against one another as whom culture says is "best" rather than what our Scriptures acknowledge best pleases God.

The rich, the educated, and the famous within our communities often are the ones who garner the pastor's attention and affection. They often have learned quite well how to get and stay on the pastor's best side and keep others at bay. But be not discouraged. Take your lesson from this example that Jesus wrought here in the eighth chapter of Luke: the rich and famous have learned how to walk with the poor(er) and infamous. That is because the kingdom of God is simply alive with people who know that their God has given them new life, life worth living, characterized by *oneness* that only He can bring! It is the work of pastors and church leaders to reexamine their church relationships, to first strike a balance in their own relationships, and allow those relationships to set a standard of inclusiveness in order to model the oneness for which our Lord called.

How good are you at math? Which principles and rules do you remember? Mathematics provides a metaphor to gain insight into this oneness as we reflect on John 17 and the Lord's priestly prayer for believers—the church—to be *one*. Each number is divisible by itself, other numbers, *and* the number one. For example, the number 12 is divisible by 1, 2, 3, 4, 6, and 12, and remains a whole number in the process. *Only* the number *one* is not divisible by any other number but *itself* and remains a whole number. There is an inherent as well as resident quantity in one.

Jesus would have grown up learning the Hebrew language where the alphabet not only had sound but also meaning and not only sound and meaning but also quantity and interesting properties that potentially convey theological realities. "That all of them may be **one**, Father, just as you are [**one**] . . . that the world may believe that you have sent me" (John 17:21, emphasis added).

Jesus wasn't asking us as believers to just *like* one another. Neither was He echoing our contemporary interracial quest, "Why can't (they) just all get along?" Jesus knew that everything in the universe is interconnected and composed by Divine Oneness. The *oneness* He had with the Father is the quality of relatedness Jesus desired for His followers.

According to Edward Hoffman, author of *The Hebrew Alphabet: A Mystical Journey*, the first Hebrew alphabet, *Aleph*, "makes no sound of its own in a word" and yet from it arises the entire alphabet of sounds . . . and meanings. Aleph represents the number one, and begins the word for Divine Unity, *Echad.*

The singleness of the number one powerfully suggests the quality of unity or divine oneness that Jesus already shared with His Father and desired to include us in. The number one possesses *indivisibility* by any other number (or power) as well as primary position. It has *position*, being the first number. In its indivisibility, it has *power*. And in its *prominence*, it becomes part of every subsequent number.

Position. The number one is the first positive number we have. Any number below it is "0"—nothingness—or diminishing negative quantity and quality. So number one is positioned at the beginning of anything that is positive. From the number one forward are all things positive. From the number one backwards are all things negative and/or to be empty of substance.

Positive. As believers, this positive substance should fill our faith and, therefore, our lives. Jesus came "that [we] might have life, and that [we] might have it more abundantly" (John 10:10 KJV); that life together with Him would be not only a wonderful experience in the hereafter but a very positive experience in the here and now! He came to add so many wonderful, positive things to our lives that there would be no room for the negative. Only sin moves us toward the negative—it literally empties out the quality of our lives! Our faith in Jesus continuously moves us into positive aspects of life "I can do all things through Christ [who] strengthen[s] me" (Philippians 4:13 KJV). This is not to say that we will not encounter some difficulties in life, but they are there to spur our growth, deepen our dependence on God, broaden our understanding about life, and enrich our faith.

Power. The power of this oneness is *the uniqueness of being divided only by itself.* It is not possible to be divided by any other number and remain whole! If it is divided by any other number, then the number one becomes a fraction, loses its quality, position, and power as an integer. It becomes a mere diminished version of itself, technically a smaller portion of what God created it or wills it to be. Now that's fine when it comes to sharing an ice-cream cone or dividing up a pizza, but it should not define the church.

Could Jesus be saying that those within the church should give up their proclivity to divide one from the other, individually or collectively? Things that often divide believers are half-truths, nuanced personal beliefs, and private agendas. Jesus is still calling us to the reality that He is far more than that. All that is in Him is far and above what can divide true believers!

I've experienced this oneness on four different continents, worshipping the Lord Jesus Christ in myriad Christian churches, tagged with myriad names overshadowing a vast array of theological beliefs and doctrinal differences. The oneness we enjoyed in worship—whether loud or quiet, solemn or joyous, seasoned with classically sung hymns or music to the beat of gospel or hip hop; whether the preaching was more rational or emotional or a blessed mixture of the two—was the same; none of that really mattered if the spirit of the Lord opened worshippers to the presence of the Lord, which leads me to the prominence of one.

Prominence. Mathematically, every subsequent number to one is enhanced because it becomes what I call "additives of one." To get two, you add one to one; to get three, you add one more, and so on. Therefore this unity of oneness becomes part of every subsequent whole number. It confirms for this believer how important it is biblically and theologically for us to add to the church via sharing of the opportunity to receive Christ rather than trying to "grow" the church through division instead.

I thank God for the Protestant Reformation that cleaved the church into its third section: Roman Catholic, Orthodox, and Protestant. However, the proliferation of denominations runs against the quality of oneness for which Jesus prayed. Within Christianity, there is room for theological and doctrinal differences, but sometimes those differences fail to bring people *to* Christ and, instead, drive people *away* from the church. How valid are the differences if they are not accomplishing the deepest desire of the One we say we love and believe in, the Lord Jesus Christ? These words hold no antidenominational sentiments, just the reality that the proliferation of denominations is not synonymous with our proclaiming the gospel around the world in the name of Him who called us to be *one*.

One problem I have witnessed in many conversations with other Christians in various congregations is that they more often know what their denomination is against rather than what it is for. Not that we shouldn't have denominations, but there has been such a proliferation, suggesting the proclivity of believers to divide instead of pursuing the spiritual oneness Jesus longed for us to have—not for our own enjoyment but as a supreme witness to the world that He has come. When we accentuate denominational beliefs, we bifurcate the sense of community and oneness that Christ prayed would characterize the people called by His name.

Conversely, when a congregation seeks to honor the Lord in worship, people of virtually any denomination can be blessed. If it is actually the Lord who is sought in worship our religious differences reflected in our styles of worship and sanctuary trappings are significantly dwarfed, which is as it should be.

Lastly, over these many years of service in the church, I have taken note that those *certain women* who know how to become one are women of authenticity. We grow up looking at everyone around us, from siblings to parents to grandparents to friends to classmates to neighbors, and so on, seeking to become what we imagine is good, appropriate, needed, or necessary for well-being in life. But there should also be a simultaneous process of *ferreting out of our lives* that which *does not feel authentic*.

Being authentic is a level of maturity that can be reached at any age! Mary Magdalene had reached a level of maturity and, I would believe, felt no need to be like Joanna, the wife of Chuza, nor Susanna, another woman of some success and notoriety within their group. What Jesus Christ had accomplished in her life had set her free not only from her past but also from her need to live in constant comparisons with others rather than concentrating on who she was as a God-made individual.

That great preacher of the nineteenth century, C. H. Spurgeon, preached a sermon entitled "Spiritual Liberty" on February 18, 1855, in celebration of what he suggested is one of God's greatest gifts to us. In that sermon, he referred not only to 2 Corinthians 3:17—"where the Spirit of the Lord is, there is freedom"—but went on to declare what we are free *from* as well as what we are free *to* as Christians. Believing that the Bible "is a never-failing treasure" of this liberty, he declares that it is "filled with boundless stores of grace." But most importantly, he asserted that as much as most folk live beyond their financial income, we fail "to live up to our spiritual income" (Spurgeon, Sermon #9). Speaking civilly, he heralded liberty as being the hallmark of religion and "the heirloom of all the sons and daughters of Adam," but to us and to Luke, even more so heirs to the gift of freedom from the Second Adam, that we "ought to live up to [this] *income, and not below it."*

eflections

Oneness is not synonymous with *sameness* because God evidently abhors sameness in that on every level of His creation and within every living species, diversity is the order of the day. What is your understanding of the oneness that Jesus yearned for among believers?

To what degree or depth do you have the capacity to celebrate someone else's good fortune?

With whom do you feel the greatest sense of competition?

*P*rayer

certain women
know the Lord's power

JESUS CALLED THE TWELVE, THE THREE, "AND OTHERS." FROM BIBLICAL Writ, Jesus declares that He does not limit His ministry to males, leaving women only on the outer boundaries. Jesus was comfortable with both. Interestingly—beyond Judas—the only problems revealed about the male disciples were primarily grounded in authority. Otherwise, they displayed few personal failings or doubts. With the one exception of Judas, their morality was never questioned nor any immorality revealed. No prevailing sins were opened up for public inspection or to ellicit compassion from fellow believers. It would seem that even Peter's declaration of fidelity and the prophetic warning of his infidelity were on a more private basis. Although his denials were in public with strangers, they had no knowledge of the prophecy of denial looming over his life. It was a private, all-knowing glance from Jesus on His way to Calvary that ushered in Peter's soul-wrenching remorse and repentance.

However, the healings, moments of deliverance, and instances of devils being cast out of Luke's *certain women* had a far more public tone and tenor. If Luke knew about them, who else also knew about them? If Luke was reporting about such maladies, did his information come only from the self-report of these women, from their testimonies, and from comments to Luke that had been made? The contrast is discernible. To the degree the Gospel writers' commentary shared about the personal lived-out experience of the Twelve with Jesus, no moral dilemmas (exceptions noted) they faced or sinful behaviors with which they struggled are part of the official report of the Gospels. Yet, at the outset, both the sinful behaviors and the moral struggles of Luke's *certain women* are "front-page" reading for the world to see.

This contrast is neither offered out of any negative perspective, lifted up as complaint, nor stated in any effort to pit females against males. Rather, it is greater assurance that these women—in no uncertain terms—experienced and knew with great depth the power of the Lord! And that all-transforming power was not hidden but was quite evident for all to see. Could that be why Jesus wanted to take them on this journey—to involve them in His wider ministry?

Whether one has learned factual data mentally, enjoyed new insights intellectually, or gained learning experientially, it cannot be taken away and often serves as preparation for what is yet to come. I believe that these women had already grown in spiritual dimensions beyond the levels of the ordinary followers of Jesus. that they were beyond the classroom of enlightened messianic conversations, that they were already beyond mountaintop moments of transfiguration. Their faith in Jesus had already succeeded in transporting them through myriad details of "what will happen to you, Jesus?" questions because they had experienced His power within their own bodies, minds, and souls!

His power was like no other. His power had broken negative holds on their lives. His power was critical to their continuing existence—without it they could not continue to live. His power activated their hope and inspired their loyalty to Him. They were readied for the journey. They, too, were ready to leave all for His sake.

Jesus brought along the Twelve who were trainable as disciples, but He brought along these *certain women* who—just by a touch of healing, an experience of deliverance, an awareness of having been set free from demonic powers—were fully ready to walk with Him as mature, well-developed disciples. Jesus needed the company of both and never ignored either as participants in the work of the kingdom. They necessitated no further assurance of the power of God in their lives. Bold, brave, brazen, even unabashed and unashamed, these *certain women* were ready to be "unleashed" unto the world for the cause of Christ!

Having worked in my church and community for over 15 years as a youth and young adult leader, by the age of 31, I was already quite well known in some Baptist circles as very personable, outgoing, and even dynamic to some degree. Amazingly, simply having crossed the state lines—moving from Virginia into Kentucky—and arriving at seminary, I was quickly labeled as "aggressive." It became a painful distortion of me as a person because, like these *certain women*, I had experienced the power of God within every area of my life. There was an assurance in place that evidently emitted "signs and signals," such as my thinking, *You have little to nothing to teach me because all that I've come to learn is already based in, rooted in, grounded in the power of God that I already know quite well.* Oh, was I in for a great surprise!

Seminary was far different than I expected and significantly different than my limited experience would have allowed my expectations to even include. The minimal expectations with which I arrived at seminary included total acceptance of a young, capable woman who had no motive but to prepare for greater service to the kingdom of our Lord. A higher level of Christian maturity is reflected in the biblical text, "Let not your good be evil spoken of" (Romans 14:16 KJV). In my naiveté, I intuited that everybody would just love me because of my lived-out exuberance for the Lord.

But those qualities put me on a cataclysmic course not only with some students, faculty, and area church leaders but, more importantly, also with myself and my faith. The experience taught me how easy it is to totally misread another soul and the relational pain that accompanies such experiences. Having been infused with encouragement, affirmation, and many opportunities to develop and be nurtured in the faith, I felt so bold and courageous, truly leaving all for the sake of the gospel and for the cause of Jesus Christ.

The most poignant piece of advice I was given by my good ole Baptist family as I was departing for seminary was this: "Don't lose your fire!" Along with the food my mother prepared and words of wisdom from a doting father, such spiritual preparation by my church family buoyed my spirit for whatever I might face in "the new world" of a "foreign" state and an unnavigated, unfathomed experience of religious training.

In these subsequent 30-plus years, I continuously encounter many female disciples who are ready to do ministry and missions not because of what a seminary professor has taught but because of what a Savior has done in their lives. I continue to be impressed by those *certain women* on the four continents I have traveled thus far, who perhaps could not defend Christianity through the formal theological constructions nor offer a systematic apologetics discourse in defense of our faith nor offer Thomas Aquinas's arguments for the existence of God. They had no need to "demythologize" Scriptures according to Rudolf Bultmann because they could so readily accept the "myths" or symbols found in biblical texts, such as heaven, hell, miracles, demons, and the like. They were in touch and in tune with the biblical Jesus who leaped off of each page of Holy Writ into the cracks, corners, and crevices of their lives, demonstrating His power over every other power present within and around them. This power that they knew urged them forward in faith, releasing them from fears of all kinds! This power enabled them to flourish even in poverty and prevail under oppression.

I'll never forget an encounter with a Palestinian woman whose house was at the foot of a hill occupied by an Israeli guard post. One would have thought that such a location would have rendered her home far more austere than it was and that life within it might seem limited by the evident and eminent threat of death sparked by the slightest provocation. Living under the presence of constant military might with someone's eyes trained to follow your every move would seem to have caused one to limit his or her enlargement of life, virtually paring it right down to the mere necessities. Not so! This woman's home, having one of the most beautiful gardens I have ever seen, would have vied for any house and garden award with one of the most beautiful gardens I have ever seen. The garden, sculptured in design and balanced in colors, had flowers blossoming in the midst of supporting foliage and proper sun and shade.

My mind raced quickly from how she had made this happen to *why* she had made this happen. I was not as interested in the how; for that, I could wait until I returned to the US and go to any landscaping class and learn some essentials in growing flowers and beautifying my yard. What I needed to glean from this woman was the secret in her spirit that allowed her to flourish under the piercing eyes of a perceived enemy and, indeed, to flourish beautifully. Then it hit me: it was not *what* she loved, but *who* she loved that made all the difference. Oh, she might have loved flowers all right—who doesn't—but many flower lovers don't have the ability to grow flowers like she did or, more importantly, the will to maintain and sustain them over the years. She did.

Her flower-growing prowess seemed to have been a testimony to the faith that provided buoyancy to her spirit, not a green thumb. This is to suggest that no matter how much oppression she lived under, what mattered was that she had the presence of the power of God to live well according to her measure of faith if not the measure of anyone else. Oh, how I rejoiced at her fortitude, boldness, brashness, and brazenness. Together they created a symphonic representation of a woman of faith that I had barely envisaged before. With only the camera of my mind's eye and the shutter clicking in my soul, that image of her in the midst of her beautiful yard, in front of a nice brick house, with the military "at the ready" as backdrop to her very existence, has remained a vivid impression 24 years has not erased.

Did she know she had a greater power within her than the power she had to endure in the presence of her world? What prompted and enabled her to dig, plant, prune, feed, weed, and arrange to her delight? What resources did she draw upon? How did she cope? Living within the volatility of the moment when the Palestinian/Israeli conflict could erupt within any given moment? When guns aimed at her and her household could begin blazing on command? What did she have that even allowed her to live under these conditions? Why didn't she move? What allowed her to stay?

Men and women of all kinds — ethnicities of every variety — have lived under pressure. Some have lived within contexts of conflict; others, with oppression for eons of time; some have floundered, and some have flourished. The difference is quite often their faith — not objectively expressed, nor intellectually disseminated, but rather experienced. Their personal, abiding experience of a God whose power knows no limit within them to heal, to deliver, and to sever demons of all kinds from their lives have made them flourish.

> Men and women of all kinds — ethnicities of every variety — have lived under pressure.

There comes a time in life when perhaps we should inquire, "What is the defining source of power in our lives?" Many people would immediately say, "God" or "Jesus Christ" or offer some other spiritually appropriate response. More importantly, the question must be, "How do we live in relationship to the power that we name in our lives?"

It is one thing to be able to name a power that is dominant in our lives, but to be able to know to what degree we live in relationship to that power is a different matter. We sing the words to "In the Garden" by C. Austin Miles — "And He walks with me and He talks with me . . ."—believing that God is always there. But to what degree are we not just aware of God's presence but able to live daily engaged in honoring, addressing, listening to, and being guided by that presence?

All too often, we want to listen to everything but God and have grown somewhat suspicious of folk who "listen" to God—those who even know His voice. It's a voice that does not make us strange to others, nor estranged from others, but enables us to be more fully engaged with others, for whom He sacrificed His life. I could rattle off a list of people I have known over the years whom I could, for a variety of reasons, have given up on relationally. That presence, that power would not let me. How I rejoice that it yet remains impossible for me.

Knowing the power of the Lord is not limited to moments of worship for *certain women*. When worship is over, the high spiritual moments are finished, or the shout is done and the songs have reached the final amen, what is the impact of that power? Part of the uniqueness of Luke's *certain women* is that they learned how to walk daily, moment by moment with that extraordinary power present within them, identifying Jesus Christ as its source. It was in the ordinary functions of their days and the ordinary happenings of their lives that they began to realize they were becoming different, stronger, better, more focused, and more useful.

Many in my day have excoriated the woman at the well. One person I heard preaching on TV made her out to be the biggest slut in human existence. I could not understand the need to demean her to that degree rather than even attempting to see her through the eyes of Jesus. Jesus never condemned her! He highlighted the choices she had made—serial monogamy—and acknowledged what she was seeking at a deeper level: water for a dry and thirsty soul.

When it comes to women in Scripture, many teachers have failed to view women through the creative purpose and intent of God or through the perspective and ministry of Jesus. Dr. John Kenney, dean of the Samuel DeWitt Proctor School of Theology at Virginia Union University has not failed to do so. He proclaimed that we have built our male/female images and relationships more on the results of sin than God's original intent. That fits the perspective that Jesus brought into His encounters with human beings. He knew we had sinned. That is why He came. He related to His Father's creation not out of the spiritual, moral, and relational devastation we had wreaked but out of the love of God that sustains us through our sin to bring us out of it. That's the redemption story.

Jesus never related to the women by judging their past, but rather from the perspective of their glorious present and promising future because of their encounter with Him. That is such a transforming perspective. If you have been praying for the salvation of friends, relatives, coworkers, or neighbors, fix in your mind images of them standing in the ordinariness of their sinful lives before the Living Christ. Allow those images to begin to upgrade your image of them, not because of what they are currently doing but out of the perspective of the soul-saving, life-changing, spirit-transforming power of the Living Christ!

Certain women throughout millennia have known they were far more than ever imagined by many people in the church. Without arrogance, ego, or chutzpah, they had an image of themselves in the throes of the power of the Living Christ—not a closed image of what they had been but the promising image of what they yet would become.

Much of Scripture interpretation has focused narrowly on females' physical elements and males' spiritual prowess, giving males dominance and authority throughout church

Jesus never ignored the certain women's participation.

history. In spite of such realistic, though disappointing, reading of church history, women have possessed the tremendous spirituality unleashed in the power of their salvation similar to that experienced by the woman at the well who, on the spot, intuited, perceived, received, and "owned" the power of the Living Christ who had told her everything . . . and to whom she surrendered everything (John 4).

Luke's Gospel "combines two major motifs," says Richard Longenecker:

> *The first has to do with the advance of the Kingdom of God. For just as conqueror invades a territory, proclaims himself as king to the existing inhabitants, and demands that they now serve him — emphasizing that he is the ruler by various shows of strength, including the defeat of any rebels who oppose him — so Jesus proclaims the arrival of God's rule in what was Satan's territory, sets free Satan's captives, and attacks Satan's allies . . . It effects the deliverance of those who were by virtue of their physical descent God's people, but had succumbed to an alien power.*

These *certain women* were proof positive that Jesus had invaded Satan's territory! Jesus never ignored the *certain women's* participation in His kingdom work. He showed His strength not in weapons of war but in delivering them from under Satan's power and control. There was no doubt as to who was now in control. They knew they were free. They knew that Jesus had unlocked and unleashed a power in them they had never known before. They were indeed free from evil domination and many human frailties because their lives had been raised to a brand-new level of power to live as originally ordained—in relationship and obedience to a holy God. That power was present in every dimension of the lives of these *certain women*. When the Lord casts out demons, He casts them out—breaks their dominance! When the Lord heals, He heals all of the disease, not half of it! When the Lord delivers, deliverance is complete. Such is the life of *certain women*.

Certain women are not worried about being "fulfilled," especially when it comes to the Lord's work. This was a major discovery for me some years ago when I was seeking spiritual counsel of a pastoral friend. After we talked, he exclaimed afterwards, "You're not fulfilled!" Had he tossed a bucket of ice water in my face, his words could not have had a more chilling effect. It was a shocking declaration but a declaration of reality that put my life in perspective. I realized he just didn't comprehend the depths of what I was sharing with him. Seeking to be fulfilled was not my aim in ministry. For me, fulfillment was simply a by-product of obedience, not a goal in and of itself.

Being less mature in the faith than he, for days thereafter, I was in emotional turmoil wondering why I wasn't "fulfilled." As those feelings evolved, they were eventually met by the power and presence of the Holy Spirit, who said to me, "God has not called you to be fulfilled but to be faithful." Being "fulfilled" is a reward, and we are not to do any of the work of the Lord for any kind of reward, personal or collective, but to faithfully offer our talents and abilities at the highest possible level, thereby bringing Him glory and honor.

For lo these many years, I've remained often unfulfilled. But for the same number of years, I have remained faithful by the grace of God and the abiding presence of the Comforter. I have discovered that being fulfilled required the attention to be focused on me, my wants, and my needs. However, I have often basked in a jubilant sense of faithfulness after teaching God's Word and seeing lives changed following an encounter with God's truth! That sense of faithfulness is far more profound than fleeting moments of fulfillment emerging from God giving me what I want rather than my heeding His call to what He wants. Ego necessitates fulfillment, whereas love for God simply necessitates faithfulness.

Marriage, children, professional success, and church status may or may not bring the fulfillment that the world tells us is our "due," but being faithful to the Lord returns dividends of fulfillment that nothing else in the world can offer. Such is the continuing element of His power to keep us faithful — of which there is no end. His power will take us from the roads in Galilee, to the foot of the Cross amid any perceived dangers, and even to a tomb — prepared for death but expecting life — and ready to tell the world, "He is not here; he is risen" (Matthew 28:6; Luke 24:6).

In the early 1970s, I yearned for models and mentors of women who served the Lord and His church. My search ultimately reconnected me with these *certain women* who were called by, and who walked with, the Lord.

eflections

Within which area of your life have you experienced the power of God?

Where in your life do you feel the greatest need for that power?

What can you do more immediately to access the power that is available to you?

*P*rayer

bibliography

Bornkamm, Gunther. *Jesus of Nazareth.* New York: Harper & Row Publishers, 1960.

Edwards, Wendy J. Deichmann. "Why God Became Man: A Gender-Inclusive Christological Perspective," *Journal of Theology.* Summer 2003.

Gardner, Paul D., ed *New International Encyclopedia of Bible Characters: The Complete Who's Who in the Bible.* Grand Rapids: Zondervan Publishing House, 1995.

Green, Joel B. *The Gospel of Luke.* The New International Commentary on the New Testament. Grand Rapids: William B. Eerdmans Publishing Company, 1997.

Hickey, Marilyn. *The Names of God.* Denver: Marilyn Hickey Ministries, 1990.

Hoffman, Edward. *The Hebrew Alphabet: A Mystical Journey.* San Francisco: Chronicle Books, 1998.

Just, Arthur A., Jr., ed. *Ancient Christian Commentary on Scripture: Luke.* Downers Grove, IL: Intervarsity Press, 2003.

Loehr, Jim, and Tony Schwartz. *The Power of Full Engagement.* New York: Free Press Paperbacks, 2003.

Longenecker, Richard N., ed. *Into God's Presence.* Grand Rapids: William B. Eerdmans Publishing Company, 2001.

Maddox, Robert. *The Purpose of Luke-Acts.* Goettingen: Vandenhoeck & Ruprecht, 1982.

Mercadante, Linda. "Winners or Whiners? Victims Caught Between Anguish and Grace." *Journal of Theology.* Summer 2003.

Metzger, Bruce M. *The New Testament: Its Background, Growth &*
    Content. 3rd ed. Nashville: Abingdon Press, 2003.

Mitchell, Henry, and Ella Mitchell. *Together for Good.* Kansas City:
    Andrews McMeel Publishing, 1999.

Moltmann-Wendel, Elisabeth. *The Women Around Jesus.* New York:
    Crossroad, 1982.

Moore, Pam Rosewell. *Life Lessons from the Hiding Place: Discovering*
    the Heart of Corrie Ten Boom. Grand Rapids: Chosen, 2004.

Newsom, Carol A., and Sharon H. Ringe, eds. *The Women's Bible*
    Commentary. Louisville: Westminster/John Knox Press, 1992.

Ogilvie, Lloyd J., gen. ed. *The Communicator's Commentary: Acts.* Waco:
    Word Books, 1983.

Phillips, J. B. *The New Testament in Modern English.* London: Geoffrey
    Bles Ltd. Publishing, 1960.

The Holy Bible. New International Version. Grand Rapids: Zondervan
    Bible Publishers, 1988.

Touch Point Bible. New Living Translation. Wheaton, IL: Tyndale
    House Publishers, Inc., 1996.

New Hope Publishers® is a division of WMU,®
an international organization that challenges Christian believers
to understand and be radically involved in God's mission.
For more information about WMU, go to www.wmu.com.
More information about New Hope books may be found
at www.newhopepublishers.com. New Hope books may be
purchased at your local bookstore.

Books to Deepen Your *Walk*

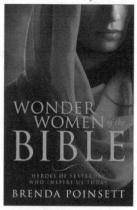

Wonder Women of the Bible
*Heroes of Yesterday
Who Inspire Us Today*
Brenda Poinsett
ISBN-10: 1-59669-094-1
ISBN-13: 978-1-59669-094-3

Directionally Challenged
*How to Find & Follow
God's Course for Your Life*
Travis Collins
ISBN-10: 1-59669-075-5
ISBN-13: 978-1-59669-075-2

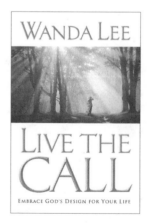

Live the Call
Embrace God's Design for Your Life
Wanda Lee
ISBN-10: 1-56309-994-2
ISBN-13: 978-1-56309-994-6

Available in bookstores everywhere

For information about these books
or any New Hope® product, visit
www.newhopepublishers.com.